Who Says?

THE
Writer's
Research

3rd Edition

Deborah H. Holdstein
Columbia College Chicago

Danielle Aquiline
Oakton Community College

New York   Oxford
Oxford University Press

Oxford University Press is a department of the University of Oxford.
It furthers the University's objective of excellence in research, scholarship,
and education by publishing worldwide. Oxford is a registered trade mark of
Oxford University Press in the UK and certain other countries.

Published in the United States of America by Oxford University Press
198 Madison Avenue, New York, NY 10016, United States of America.

© 2020 by Oxford University Press

For titles covered by Section 112 of the US Higher Education
Opportunity Act, please visit www.oup.com/us/he for the latest
information about pricing and alternate formats.

Library of Congress Cataloging-in-Publication Data
Names: Holdstein, Deborah H., 1952- author. | Aquiline, Danielle, author.
Title: Who says? : the writer's research / Deborah H Holdstein, Columbia
    College Chicago, Danielle Aquiline, Oakton Community College.
Description: Third edition. | New York : Oxford University Press, [2021] |
    Includes bibliographical references and index. | Summary: "Now in a new
    edition, Who Says? The Writer's Research is an innovative and brief
    research guide focusing on information literacy. The text shows students
    not only how to do research but also why research is important. Written
    for today's college student, Who Says? addresses contemporary research
    issues head on: —What does it mean to conduct research in an age when
    we are bombarded by collaborative information through online media and
    databases like Wikipedia? —Who owns this information? How do we know?
    —As information circulates and changes, do the lines between audience
    and author blur? —How should these changes alter our expectations as
    readers and as writers? By prompting students to think critically about
    matters of ownership and authority, Who Says? not only shows students
    how to find and incorporate credible sources in their writing, but also
    encourages students to synthesize their own ideas with the ideas of
    others, leading them to develop more confident and compelling voices as
    writers"— Provided by publisher.
Identifiers: LCCN 2020004437 (print) | LCCN 2020004438 (ebook) | ISBN
    9780197525494 (paperback) | ISBN 9780197525500 (epub) | ISBN
    9780197525517 (ebook)
Subjects: LCSH: Research—Methodology—Study and teaching
    (Higher)—Handbooks, manuals, etc. | Report writing—Study and teaching
    (Higher)—Handbooks, manuals, etc. | Academic writing—Handbooks,
    manuals, etc.
Classification: LCC LB2369 .H64 2021 (print) | LCC LB2369 (ebook) | DDC
    808.02—dc23
LC record available at https://lccn.loc.gov/2020004437
LC ebook record available at https://lccn.loc.gov/2020004438

Printing number: 9 8 7 6 5 4 3 2
Printed by Sheridan Books, Inc.,
United States of America

contents

Contents

Contents

preface

In 2008, *The Atlantic* published Nicholas Carr's "Is Google Making Us Stupid?" in which the author argues that our frequent use of the Internet is causing physiological changes to our brains, with great impact on the way we read and engage with texts. The piece seemed to strike a chord, quickly becoming popular; the piece was later anthologized in *The Best American Science Writing*. In explaining how his own reading habits and abilities have noticeably changed, Carr notes, "Once I was a scuba diver in the sea of words. Now I zip along the surface like a guy on a jet ski."

We have been using this metaphor as a touchstone to address the ways in which *Who Says? The Writer's Research* will engage in the kinds of conversations necessary for contemporary first-year writing classrooms and beyond—conversations missing from current research textbooks. Carr's metaphor has helped us shape our book, and it speaks, we think, to the varying challenges faced by current writing students (and, in turn, writing teachers). Namely, how does accountable, rich, and scholarly research exist alongside technologies like Google and Wikipedia that often oversimplify information? And, further, how can we push our students to engage deeply with scholarly resources when they are becoming increasingly involved—or, debilitated, as Carr seems to argue—by their own engagement with new media?

As the title *Who Says?* indicates, we are interested in helping students grapple with how and when they rely on source material to synthesize their own ideas. *Who Says?* intends to get students thinking about questions of authority and ownership and about what it means to do research writing in an age when we are all bombarded by collaborative information via databases such as Wikipedia. We want our students to be smart in the ways in which they approach writing and in the ways in which they approach reading and sourcing information.

Through our own experiences as instructors, we note that many students still seem to leave our first-year writing classes with little if any notion of why we conduct or write about research to begin with. Unlike many of the books we have used and read, *Who Says?* synthesizes the strengths of these books and fosters students' synthesis of ideas, rather than offering the kind of "cut and paste" strategy so often present in many research textbooks. The first several chapters of *Who Says?* also engage in global conversations about the nature of research writing, addressing as well the writer's important role in academic conversations. In addition, each chapter in the book is punctuated by a section titled "Ideas into Practice." New in this third edition—along with updates to MLA and APA citation requirements—is a section on "Misinformation and Fake News"; enhanced information and useful tips about effective presentations and the visuals accompanying them; and, in each chapter, a section titled "Stop and Consider," which highlights aspects of particular topics and asks readers to apply the tenets to their own work.

Who Says? is primarily intended for use in first-year writing courses, but we have repeatedly seen its relevance and usefulness to writing-intensive and writing-in-the-disciplines courses as well. It's important to note, however, what we cannot accomplish in a volume intended to be brief and readily accessible: highly detailed information about incorporating multimedia resources into research projects (particularly since such information becomes dated so quickly), although such information has been augmented in this new edition; information about specific research methodologies or discipline-specific techniques that are more appropriately conveyed by the course instructor; the many complex nuances of Internet searches, as it would be impossible to address every database and every search engine (especially as they are sometimes ephemeral); and the entire range of bibliographical citation formats, although we do delineate the major formats and point writers toward currently reliable online sources. And while we spend a good deal of time emphasizing the formulation of a strong argument and thesis and the accountability with which they are defended, this is not an argument book per se, as this is well beyond the purview of this volume.

Instead, *Who Says?* offers student writers a companion to in-class and instructor-assigned work toward the preparation of a successful and accountable papers that involve the use of sources—whether the extensive, traditional research paper or the shorter essay. It's concise, with checklists and bullet points—along with careful explanation, where appropriate—and aims to accompany other texts and valuable work in a given course and afterward.

New to this Edition

- Updated MLA and APA style standards
- Expanded coverage of the multimodal forms of research presentations
- Revised examples of research papers
- Augmented assignments and activities throughout each chapter
- Updated "The Wikipedia Problem" to reflect more relevant conversations about "fake news" and the pitfalls of doing research online
- Expanded list of sample research paper topics
- Added, new "Stop and Consider" conversation breakouts in each chapter

About the Authors

Deborah H. Holdstein is a Dean of the School of Liberal Arts and Sciences and Professor of English at Columbia College Chicago

Danielle Aquiline is Professor of English at Oakton Community College

acknowledgments

We appreciate our colleagues at Oxford University Press, USA, notably Steve Helba, whose enthusiasm for this project and for our authorship deserves (and receives) our gratitude. He is a wonderful, responsive editor. We also thank Kora Fillet for her troubleshooting and helpfulness. It is a privilege to work with OUP.

Columbia College Chicago and Oakton Community College also loom large in their support for this book, and we thank the numerous colleagues who directly or indirectly offered access to photocopiers, scanners, and the like.

Our personal thank-yous are profound and simple: Deborah and Danielle thank Jay Boersma and Sona Patel, respectively, for deep and unyielding support for any and all projects and ventures. We also acknowledge our children: Danielle's Finn and Elias, and Deborah's Emily and David.

We also wish to acknowledge Craighton Berman for his inspired Sketchnote illustrations found throughout the book. We also thank David Gilman for his help with the original index.

As is the custom of a credible publisher, OUP consulted with colleagues at diverse institutions across the United States for their feedback on this project. We, too, would also like to thank the following reviewers whose insights helped guide us through the revision process for the first edition: Kathryn T. Adams, Allan Hancock College; Lynn Alexander, University of Tennessee-Martin; Deborah Coxwell Teague, Florida State University; Jeanne Daningburg, Roberts Wesleyan College; Jason DePolo, North Carolina A&T State University; Emily Dial-Driver, Rogers State University; Anthony Edgington, University of Toledo; Kim Gainer, Radford

University; Blake Hobby, University of North Carolina-Asheville; Kathleen Mollick, Tarleton State University; Robin Lee Mozer, University of Louisville; Van Piercy, Lone Star College-Tomball; Alison Reynolds, University of Florida; Cary D. Ser, Miami Dade College-Kendall; Keith Sisson, University of Memphis; Marilyn Stachenfeld, Saddleback College; Colette Tennant, Corban University; and Matthew Wilsey-Cleveland, University of Colorado, Boulder. And thank you as well to all those reviewers who advised us for the second edition: James Allen, College of DuPage; Monique Bos, Georgia Southern University; Christie Cognevich, Louisiana State University; Nancy Comorau, Ohio Wesleyan University; Sonia Delgado-Tall, City Colleges of Chicago—Kennedy-King College; Emily Dial-Driver, Rogers State University; Regina Dilgen, Palm Beach State College; Sonia Feder-Lewis, Saint Mary's University of Minnesota; Melanie Kisthardt, Immaculata University; Mary Beth Kwenda, Black Hills State University; Abigail Montgomery, Blue Ridge Community College; Denise Ortiz, Walla Walla Community College; Leslie Roberts, Oakland Community College; Cary Ser, Miami-Dade College; Debra Silverman, Ulster County Community College; Jermaine Singleton, Hamline University; Keith Sisson, Memphis; Linda Uhlenkott, Great Basin College; Heather Urbanski, Fitchburg State University; Angela Williamson, University of Wisconsin—Fox Valley; and Robert Wilson, Juilliard School. And for the third edition: James Allen, College of DuPage; Kelly L. Bezio, Texas A&M University-Corpus Christi; Nicholas Hoffman, Ohio State University; Yvette Michelle Koepke-Nelson, University of Dakota; Moumin Manzoor Quazi, Tarleton State University; Cary D. Ser, Miami-Dade College; and Jill Marie Treftz, Marshall University.

CHAPTER one

What Is Information?

The Internet is the world's largest library. It's just that all the books are on the floor.
        —*John Allen Paulos*

If you peruse a variety of websites, including that of the University of Rhode Island Library (http://www.uri.edu/library/staff_pages/kinnie/lib120/info.html), you will see how difficult it is to find agreement on the definition of *information*, as the following three quotes that were on an earlier version of that site indicate. And interestingly, since the first edition of this book was published, the information *about* this information is no longer available on that website, pointing to the ever-changing, fluid nature of information that is not in traditional print:

> All ideas, facts and imaginative works of the mind which have been communicated, recorded, published and/or distributed formally or informally in any format.
> —*American Library Association*

> In the beginning there was information. The word came later. The transition was achieved by the development of organisms with the capacity for selectively exploiting this information in order to survive and perpetuate their kind.
> —*Fred Dreske, Knowledge and the Flow of Information (Bedford Books, 1981)*

> Data becomes information only when it's put into a context.
> —*John McChesney, reporter, National Public Radio*

Information and Being Literate about Information

As citizens and as consumers, it is essential that we become articulate investigators (some might say "critical thinkers") of that which is represented as information, especially allegedly accurate, authoritative information. This is what the term "information literacy" is about. For instance, if, indeed, the poet Gertrude Stein was correct in saying,

"Everybody gets so much information all day long that they lose their common sense," it is even more striking that this statement was attributed to Stein (according to a website that we shall not mention) as having been said in 1959.

This is interesting for several reasons, and it illustrates the importance of being literate about information. First, as you can imagine, the "information overload," as it is commonly called, has only increased exponentially since 1959, and even more so since the advent of the Internet, so Stein's words (if, indeed, they are) ring especially true today. Second: In Stein's era, and despite her otherwise playful use of language, it is highly unlikely that Stein would have used the plural "they" as the pronoun referring to the singular "everybody." In this context, she likely would have written as follows: "... he loses his common sense," as was common usage of the time. The third reason: Stein died in 1946, making it impossible for her to have pronounced much of anything in 1959.

This tells us two significant things about information and the importance of being literate when confronted with various types of information—and about this information in particular. First, there is difference among information, accurate information, and real knowledge. And, second, there is always a need to attribute and cite information accurately and carefully.

Stop and Consider

Have a conversation about a time when you realized that you have fallen prey to inaccurate information on the Internet, whether it's an untruthful announcement about a celebrity's demise, a "too good to be true" sales offer for something everyone's trying to buy, or a pyramid scheme (such as "essential oils," "skin care lines," "colorful leggings," and so forth). We've all been there. With the benefit

(continued)

of hindsight, what should all of us do differently? What clues might there be, and how should we proceed when the clues are not very evident?

The United States National Forum on Information Literacy defines "information literacy" as "the ability to know when there is a need for information, to be able to identify, locate, evaluate, and effectively use that information for the issue or problem at hand" (infolit. org, United States Government, a site that, sadly, no longer exists). This is in great measure what *Who Says?* is about.

Although the philosophical distinctions among information literacy, information, and knowledge are perhaps beyond our purpose here, we have written *Who Says? A Writer's Research* to help you begin the important process of writing about topics that require research. This book will accompany the wisdom of your instructor and other documents or texts she or he might choose for your course and assignment, and it is not meant to be a comprehensive, highly detailed manifesto on any and all forms of research writing. (Indeed, you will note that we often use the words "research essay" and "research paper" interchangeably, even though the former represents a more personal type of research project and the latter represents a more academic research venture. We want to be inclusive of the varieties of assignments you might encounter.)

Initiating Conversation

What questions should you ask about information that you read or see online or that is communicated via Twitter, for instance? Reflect on a time when you heard about or noticed incorrect information online or otherwise in the media. Was it about politics? A celebrity? A current global or national event? Describe the event and analyze the ways in which you could or could not discern whether the information was reliable. What made you suspicious? How did you research or otherwise discover information that seemed correct on the same subject?

Being Overwhelmed—This Is a Process?

All types of research—whether a major, federally funded project or a term paper assignment—are characterized by a process, that is, a set of procedures or methods by which the research assignment, in this case, is carried out.

For instance, you've likely heard about the process for scientific research, by which scientists establish a problem, examine aspects of the problem using prior information, create a hypothesis, compose a research methodology, and then set about proving (and sometimes disproving) the hypothesis. Your task, although not necessarily scientific, is similar. As you will see as you go through these chapters and use the guidance of your instructor, you will examine what interests you; find ways to center and focus what interests you; see what information has been established by others who are interested in the topic; perhaps create your own, relevant research materials (such as interviews, if appropriate for your investigation); craft an argument; and prove that argument in writing.

This is to say that while you might be feeling overwhelmed by the laundry list of tasks that lie ahead, the good news is that there is, in fact, a process—a series of tried-and-true steps that, no matter how recursive or repetitive they may seem, are steps that you eventually will incorporate into the idiosyncrasies and complexities of your own research project. In learning any new process, you might find these steps cumbersome; however, we find that they become second nature after a while, and you will find your comfort level increase as you become more intellectually secure with and accountable for the complexities of your project.

This book is therefore intended as a supportive guide, one to accompany you as you begin to think about and formulate a topic, generate resources, craft a thesis/statement of purpose, and fulfill the other obligations of an appropriately documented, well-crafted written research project. We hope that you will use the *information* you gather on your particular topic to generate *knowledge*, as you discern that which is useful, credible, and appropriate for your audience and for the work that you intend to do.

Ideas Into Practice

This is one of many ways to develop a game plan and timeline for your research and writing. After all, it's always good to have a game plan, and the research process is no different.

With the help of the deadlines and other requirements set by your instructor, create a timeline for your work, whether it's on hard copy in a notebook or on your smartphone, tablet, or laptop calendar. First, create a list of milestones; this might include "determine topic," "vet sources," "craft thesis," "create annotated bibliography," "annotated bibliography due for class discussion," and so forth. If one of your entries is "find topic by September 30," you'll likely want to insert into your calendar (print or otherwise) a reminder two weeks before that deadline.

Work with your fellow classmates and your instructor to determine and record milestones that will be common to everyone, adapting them and your own work habits to ensure that your work is completed well and on time.

CHAPTER two

Says Who? The Writer's Authority, the Writer's Voice

talking points

- How does the rhetorical situation affect the way I approach my work?
- What is ethos?
- Why is my ethos as a researcher important?
- What helps me to establish my ethos? How can my ethos be damaged?
- What is voice?
- Where does my voice as a writer come in?
- Does my diction matter?

We would like you to think about the various situations in which you might be asked to produce written text, situations that will almost certainly extend beyond the classroom. Clearly, these points are likely useful to you for your research writing in addition to other occasions for writing. Because you likely will be asked to write in a variety of ways and for many different audiences throughout both your educational and professional careers, it is important that you always consider the *rhetorical situation* for which you are writing.

The Rhetorical Situation

The *rhetorical situation*—a concept attributed to Aristotle—asks us to consider the following when composing a written text: the writer, the audience, the purpose, the topic, and the occasion. Let's break this down even further and take a look at the kinds of questions that will help you address each of those elements.

Considering the Writer—Or, as Aristotle Put It, the Speaker

Who is the speaker? How does she or he convey authority? Does the speaker work to develop ethos? What is the experience of the speaker and how does that experience award the speaker credibility?

Considering the Audience—Your Readers

Who is the target audience for your argument? What does the audience expect? Does the audience consist of experts in the field of study? Will the audience be evaluating the written text in any way? What is the audience's relationship to the writer?

Considering the Purpose—In Addition to Fulfilling the Assignment

Is the piece of writing meant to convey a message? Make a point? Entertain? Delight? Praise? Criticize? Analyze? Is the writing trying to persuade us of something? What is the goal?

Considering the Topic—Larger Issues

Is the tone of the writing appropriate for this topic? What are the specific conventions for the particular discipline in which you are writing? Does the writing provide the necessary context for the argument being made?

Considering the Occasion

Why is this piece of writing being composed? In what context will this writing be presented? What are the expectations and standard conventions of that particular context? What is the setting for this writing (time, place, etc.)?

These considerations lead to our discussion of *ethos*.

Establishing Ethos

In addition to the rhetorical situation, we think it's important to remember that research writing is an intellectual activity. What we're thinking about won't necessarily transmit a specific set of skills, but we hope to make you aware of the larger contexts for writing and for writing the results of your research.

To further contextualize this conversation, we need to talk a bit more about *rhetoric*. So let's do it this way:

> *Quick Fact*
> Aristotle defined rhetoric as the "art of persuasion" and identified three primary rhetorical modes: pathos, logos, and ethos.

For the purpose of this discussion, we'll have to be satisfied with rather quick definitions. Although we'll talk primarily about ethos, let us introduce you to these basic concepts (see Table 2.1).

Table 2.1   THE THREE MAIN FORMS OF RHETORIC

Pathos—Appealing to the audience on the basis of emotion.	**Logos**—Appealing to the audience on the basis of logic.	**Ethos**—Appealing to the audience on the basis of one's character and implied, guiding beliefs.
Beliefs Feelings Emotion Subjectivity	Logic Reason Fact Objectivity	Reputation Trustworthiness Authority Credibility

Let's put some of this into action. Let's say that you want to persuade your family that you should be given an all-expense-paid trip to Europe next summer. (We know. This is just an exercise, remember?)

Now, make an appeal to your parents (or to other persons to whom you plan to appeal), using each of the three forms of rhetoric: pathos, logos, and ethos.

Using Pathos

"But all my friends are going, and don't you want me to have important life experiences?" or "Do you want me to be the only one of my friends who doesn't get to go on this trip?"

Using Logos

"Sixty percent of students who travel abroad are more readily accepted into professional and graduate schools. I have documented evidence that an overseas experience will not only increase the depth and breadth of my knowledge, but also that it will provide the kind of cross-cultural benefits that employers look for these days."

Demonstrating Ethos

"I've received good grades all of last year, and I'm on the Honor Roll. I've proven myself to be personally responsible, as my exemplary behavior during spring break last year amply illustrates. I'm responsible, I can multitask and experience the world while getting my work done, and I'm dedicated to making you and our family proud."

Let us emphasize that your real-life situations will, of course, be far more nuanced and not nearly this simple. You'll likely be relying on a combination of these forms for your arguments, whether for your family or for your writing.

However, we want you to be most mindful of your ethos, because both pathos and logos, depending on how these are demonstrated, both affect your ethos—that is, the good character you project as a credible speaker or writer. To put it even more simply, does your targeted audience have good reason to believe or want to follow the argument you are making?

Ways to Damage Your Ethos

Sometimes the little things—or, rather, things that seem little to you—can have a tremendous impact on your ability to impress or persuade your reader and could potentially undermine your ethos.

Let's say you're watching a press conference featuring a prominent politician. He or she is less than prepared and seems evasive when asked questions that would have seemed to be central to the reason for the conference in the first place. This might indicate to you that either the politician is refusing to answer honestly or that he or she just doesn't know the answer. What would be your reaction? Such stances clearly damage the ethos of the speaker. Would it help your perception of the politician for him or her to have simply said, "I cannot answer this question because I do not yet know the answer," rather than trying to be evasive? For most of us, yes.

The point here is that even if you previously haven't heard of the word *ethos*, you might have called into question the credibility of the politician. You are aware of speakers' trustworthiness and your perception of that trustworthiness even if you haven't been aware of the Greek term for "character."

Let's think about how this figures into your ethos as a writer.

For instance, if you rely too heavily on source materials (the kind of "patchwriting" we'll discuss later on in these pages), you may communicate that you as a research writer don't fully understand and can't support your own argument without back-to-back quoting of others. On the other hand, if you present information that isn't cited carefully—and that isn't common knowledge—your audience will question how you know this information and will begin to suspect that you might be plagiarizing or, at the very least, that you do not know how to document appropriately and properly.

If your article isn't formatted appropriately—if it doesn't follow the format or the appropriate conventions of the discipline in which you're writing—these issues also complicate and undermine your credibility as a writer and thinker.

In the end, think also about the signs and signals that mark a credible source as you conduct research and the things you see that might discredit a particular source, thus damaging your own credibility. For example, consider a Web page that is completely user-made without documented, research-worthy materials. Using this as an authoritative source potentially makes you less than authoritative, unless, of course, your topic is "wonky websites."

Again, although you may not be familiar with the term *ethos*, you likely are well able to identify or discern a credible website in the first five to ten seconds of the site's loading on your screen, further indicating that there is a variety of nuanced signals that audiences note and use to conclude whether a website, politician, or research paper is credible and authoritative. It's your voice that comes through that research paper—and it's your ethos that is conveyed through your voice and choice of diction.

Initiating Conversation

Think about the rhetorical situation of an advertisement, either print, online, or on television. We suspect that a Super Bowl ad from Chipotle Restaurants will have a long life on YouTube. Find this animated "Scarecrow" ad online, and analyze the rhetorical situation: Who is the intended audience? How do you know? What visual elements contribute to the ad's effect? Why is there music but no dialogue? What are the occasion and context for this ad? What argument does the ad make? (Was this meant to "go viral"? How can you tell?) What do these elements say about the context in which the ad was created and the audience for whom it might have been intended? Would this ad appeal to others besides the intended audience? Why or why not? Would anything have to change, or not? Think about what you've just read regarding the three main forms of rhetoric—pathos, logos, and ethos. How are these put to use in the ad?

If for some reason this ad is no longer available, choose another advertisement and, similarly, analyze the rhetorical situation.

Voice and Writing

When we speak of "voice," we don't mean the way you sound when you speak. Instead, we're talking about the unique way that you convey your individual style as a writer. Many factors come into the reader's sense of your voice: your word choice (diction), your turn of phrase (your syntax), or the sophistication of your vocabulary (and knowing when not to sound overinflated or deliberately obscuring).

Think of the blogs you read regularly, for example. In an era of online text, bloggers must work especially hard to hone their individual voices; they must write in a way that both effectively communicates their personalities and sets them apart from the sea of other bloggers with whom they are competing for your readership.

We are both avid readers of food blogs and can readily identify our favorite bloggers by their written voices. In fact, it is often the voice—the choices these writers have made in the way they write— that attract us to their blogs in the first place, and it's the voice that keeps us coming back time and time again. Their voices are distinctively *theirs*. That is, they are easily identifiable and help us, the readers, better understand who each person is as a writer (or food blogger) and what she or he wants us to understand as readers (or foodie fans).

Consider this example from the popular blog *Smitten Kitchen* (www.smittenkitchen.com):

> *It's the first week of January, so I am going to go out on a limb and guess that no fewer than 52 percent of you are gnawing on a carrot stick right now. If you're not gnawing on a carrot stick right now, you probably have some within reach of you. If they're not within reach of you, they're in your fridge, because you, like most of us, are more ambitious when it comes to grocery lists than you might be when it's time to consume said groceries. And if they're not in your fridge, you might have them on your mind, nagging at you. Early January is like that. (Late January is all about rich comfort foods. Trust me.)*
> *—(January 2013)*

In this excerpt from this very successful blog, writer Deb Perelman demonstrates a certain "I know you, you trust me, and I'm your best buddy" voice that has—in addition to outstanding recipes and a compelling "backstory" ("Regular Woman Works Miracles in Tiny Manhattan Kitchen," the headline might read)—contributed to her success. Perelman knows that even if you do not find yourself "gnawing on a carrot stick," even if you don't have any in your refrigerator, as she seems to assume, you will intuitively understand what it means for her to begin this part of her blog by stating, "It's the first week in January." What does that mean to most readers? Probably the post-holiday slump of back to work in (often) terrible weather, (for many) cold temperatures, a possible need to curb one's food intake after the holidays, and a desire to hibernate until spring. Perlman doesn't need to say all this, of course: she assumes you, the reader, get it, even if her assumptions about you are incorrect. And because her voice is so familiar, when the excerpt ends with a request that you trust her, it's likely that you will; and even if you're not sure, you'll likely give the recipe a try (and *then* you'll trust her). Perelman's voice reveals warmth, closeness, and an intelligent, welcoming friendship—an intimate acquaintance who's talking with you across the kitchen table.

Of course, it's unlikely that you will be writing for an audience of foodies who you'll be able to assume are your best friends—ever. Nonetheless, it is still important that, when conceiving your writing and your paper, you are mindful of your audience and your purpose so that your voice is appropriate for your particular rhetorical situation. Depending on the subject and writer, another blog, of course, will have a completely different tone and effect on the reader. In research writing—and again, depending on the discipline or genre in which you're writing—your voice may come across as personal or too personal; stiff or not stiff enough; scholarly or too informal. You get the picture.

Let's say that you want to communicate to several people the fact that you're under the weather and will have to miss class. The way in which you communicate this will depend not only on the medium and genre of your communication but also on your targeted audience:

For the instructor, via e-mail:

> *Dear Professor Hogwash: I'm really sorry, but I'm running a fever, and I won't be able to be in class today. I will follow the syllabus, and I will be sure to prepare this assignment for our next class, and if it is acceptable to you, I will also turn in the work that we were to have done in class today. As we are advised on the syllabus, I will also contact a classmate to see if there is anything new that comes in class today. Sincerely, Smart Student*

For a classmate/friend, via text message:

> *Hey. Dipping stats today. Txt me aftr Hog's class with info and hw. Ttyl.*

Clearly, you would not, we trust, use text-messaging-appropriate or informal language when communicating with your instructor.

Now, these are extreme examples, but as with the exercise regarding the different forms of rhetoric, your voice depends on your targeted audience and the medium and level of diction (word choice) you invoke. These are decisions that you make on a daily basis, but we'd like you to be mindful of these choices, especially as they have an impact on your research and your writing. Part of your job as a writer—and part of your responsibility in making your essay readable, persuasive, and cohesive—is to find the proper voice with which you will write. Doing so is often a balance, not between the extremes we illustrated earlier, but rather in knowing how to use appropriate word choice and the style that's expected in the genre and discipline in which you are writing, balancing citation with your own use of language. Keep in mind, of course, that each of your sources will have the author's own distinct voice, so your primary struggle will be to ensure that your voice as a research writer sets an appropriate tone for your paper.

Stop and Consider

All of us engage in something we might call "code-switching," whether it's adjusting our vocabulary to suit particular audiences, for instance, or modifying our reactions depending on the situation, as you can see in the e-mail-versus-text example in the previous pages. What turns of phrase have you used in essays in the past that you might not use in everyday conversation—and the reverse? For instance, while we might write "F2F" (meaning "face to face") in a text, it probably won't fly in a formal essay—or even for an e-mail at work, depending on the purpose and audience of that email.

Look at your last essay assignment and some of your own texts. What other examples can you think of?

Owning Your Voice

In the process of integrating their source materials, some students lose sight of their own distinct voices and their own arguments. The important point is this: although you are looking to researchers and scholars to help you construct your argument, this is ultimately your work and your research writing should represent who you are both as an academic and as a writer. We treat this topic further elsewhere in this book.

Ideas Into Practice

Think of the example we gave you about your request to spend the summer in Europe. In that example, we asked you to use each of the three rhetorical forms in an attempt to persuade. Now, choose one of the research topics from the following list and enact a similar exercise in which you try to persuade your audience using these three forms. Therefore, in this activity, proceed as follows:

> After choosing the topic, take a stand on that topic. Remember that your stand must be something that can be argued—it cannot suggest a "yes" or "no" response. Consider your audience. What do you need to do to appeal to that particular audience or set of audiences?

> As an intellectual exercise, make an appeal using each of the three rhetorical forms—ethos, logos, pathos—as discussed in this chapter.

This is an opportunity to try out your research skills, which we will discuss elsewhere in this book, as you find the best examples with which to argue your point of view. The topics: *These are deliberately controversial (and somewhat hackneyed, but not necessarily unimportant) topics, ones that your instructor might dissuade you from choosing for your research paper. (And we'll leave that to the instructor to explain.)*

Marijuana legalization
Abortion rights
Gun control
Euthanasia
Animal rights

CHAPTER three

But You Said This Was Collaborative: Plagiarism

talking points

- What is plagiarism?
- How do I know when I'm plagiarizing?
- I can just change the words, right?
- What are the various forms of plagiarism?
- How do I document the information if it can be considered common knowledge? Should I still account for it?
- What are some ways to avoid plagiarism?

In Chapter 2, you read a great deal about determining who you are as a writer and how you can work to establish your *ethos*—your credibility as a researcher. It is important that you realize that your ethos is dependent not only on what ideas you contribute to academic conversations but also on how indebted and accountable you are to the ideas that came before you. In many ways, this is the dance that all researchers must do: balancing the work they are doing with the work that others—often many others—have already done.

Understanding Plagiarism

It is amid this choreography that students often get caught in the trap of plagiarism. Intentionally or unintentionally, students will lose sight of their own voices and ideas and will, instead, misappropriate the words and language of their resources—that is, the words written and published by others.

Plagiarism occurs when you use words or ideas that are not your own and you do not cite them. In other words, you plagiarize when you do not acknowledge in appropriate ways that someone else has written words or has published ideas that you claim are yours. You plagiarize by doing the following:

- Stealing another's ideas or words and passing them off as your own
- Using resources without giving credit
- Forgetting to put quotation marks around a direct quote
- Buying an essay and turning it in as your own

Deliberate plagiarizing violates academic integrity and is nothing short of cheating. It is admitting that you—the research writer—are incapable of crafting your own essay; it is also an admission of defeat. And, in many colleges and universities, plagiarism is seen, in many ways, as a moral offense punishable by suspension or expulsion.

Regardless of whether you copy from a published or private source, a website or a magazine, an encyclopedia or an Internet forum, unless you give credit to other authors for both their ideas and their words, you have plagiarized. Be mindful, as well, of copyright laws, particularly as research projects are sometimes written as well as multimedia: graphics, photographs, music sampling, and the like are all subject to forms of copyright. You must credit all sources to avoid copyright infringement, even if you are using an image, say, only for your presentation.

Furthermore, keep in mind that, although the Internet has certainly made it easier to find sources and essays to plagiarize, it has also made it easier for teachers to detect plagiarism. Websites such as *WriteCheck*, *TurnItIn*, and *iThenticate* have developed what some institutions and professors find to be useful tools that aid in both plagiarism detection and prevention. However, as teachers, we also recognize that students sometimes plagiarize accidentally. In most instances, the penalties—and the violation of ethics—are equally severe, even if the plagiarism is inadvertent. So, in what follows, we hope to equip you with tools that will help you to avoid the plagiarism trap.

Examples of Plagiarism

The following is an excerpt from Paul Shepard's essay "Hunting and Human Values." We've used this passage, and the samples following, to illustrate various kinds of plagiarism:

Original Text

Regardless of the technological advance, man remains part of a dependent upon nature. The necessity of signifying and recognizing this relationship remains, though it may not seem so. The hunter is our agent of awareness. He is not only an observer but a participant and receiver. He knows that man is a member of a natural community and that the processes of nature will never become so well understood or controlled that faith will cease to be important.

> —Shepard, Paul. "Hunting and Human Values."
> Man in the Landscape: A Historic View of the
> Esthetics of Nature, 190–213. Athens: University
> of Georgia Press, 2002.

Word-for-Word Plagiarism

Paul Shepard suggests that the hunter is not only an observer but also a participant and receiver. The hunter knows that man is a member of a natural community and that the processes of nature will never become so well understood or controlled that faith will cease to be important.

This kind of exact copying and pasting is the most blatant form of plagiarism, even if it is unintended. Although the original author, Paul Shepard, has been acknowledged and the quote attributed to him, there has been no attempt to designate this passage as a direct quote or to document the source from which these ideas came. There should be both quotation marks around a passage of more than four lines of prose or more than three lines of poetry and an appropriate citation, using a recognized citation format (usually specified by your instructor).

Patchwork, or the Plagiarism Paraphrase
Man is dependent upon nature, regardless of the technological advance. Though it doesn't seem like it, the necessity of signifying and recognizing this relationship still remains. Man is not only an observer; he is also a participant and receiver (Shepard 5).

This is the kind of plagiarism to which students fall prey most often. It is important to note that, while there is a citation form (using the MLA style) here, *this passage is still plagiarized*.

Often, this sort of plagiarism is the result of inadequate paraphrasing, and that is the case here. Students may think they are translating ideas from a text into their own language, but they are really just shuffling around the text's original language. When there are three or more words linked together in the same order as the original text, such as "regardless of the technological advance" or "the necessity of signifying and recognizing the relationship still remains," the phrase should be crafted as a direct quote, with the writer surrounding the passage with quotation marks.

Idea-Based Plagiarism
The hunter is a necessity; he is our only agent of awareness. He is there to remind us that we are part of a larger natural community. No matter how technologically advanced we become, we will always be dependent on nature.

This is an example of the way particular ideas are still explicitly derived from the original text, even though the writer may have changed aspects of the language. This example also illustrates how plagiarizing extends beyond just blatant copying; idea-based plagiarism is a less explicit form of stealing, but it is unethical and irresponsible nonetheless.

Therefore, just as you would with a direct quote, you must include appropriate, academic documentation that credits the author.

Stop and Consider

As with all information in this book, and as we've indicated, these strategies apply not only to your class work, but also to your life in the world. That is, students aren't the only ones who have been accused of plagiarism.

As a learning experience, team up with a classmate and research well-known people who have been accused of "borrowing" language or texts from others. Compare the original with the suspect piece. What can you learn from this comparison? Given that many people can certainly discuss or write about the same type of topic or theme, how might the borrower have either rephrased or credited the original?

Avoiding Plagiarism

The first step in avoiding plagiarism involves making a commitment. Writers must commit to doing the work necessary to integrate resources properly and to use those resources to synthesize new and original ideas. Once that commitment is made, avoiding plagiarism is actually fairly simple; be a diligent note taker and a savvy editor. We can help with both of those highly nuanced tasks, and we trust that the examples from Paul Shepard's work are a start.

It's Okay to Use Resources (and It's Expected)

Using resources doesn't diminish your credibility as a writer; it actually *enhances* your credibility. *How* you use them is important.

Quite often, students fail to realize that research is a collaborative process, but it's collaborative in a variety of ways, some of which might not be anticipated. You, as the writer, are collaborating with the ideas of many others who have done similar or related work before you. And guess what? Those scholars—the very ones that *you* are citing—likely once depended on the work of others, too. This is how the conversation continues, and this is the way that academic communities operate.

When you cite resources in research writing, you demonstrate to your reader several important things:

- You have done time in the trenches. That is, you've spent hours, days, or perhaps weeks searching through online databases, thumbing through online (or, very rarely these days, hard copy) card catalogs and requesting materials, and perusing shelves or lists of books in the library. In other words, you've done your research, and appropriate documentation proves it.
- You value the academic contribution of scholars. You see worth in work done by others, and you understand that consulting the ideas of others is an integral part of formulating your own ideas.

- You are concerned about your own ethos. You want to be able to appear credible, responsible, and ethical.
- You are savvy enough not only to quote from, but also engage with, your resources.

Therefore, don't be afraid to rely on your resources as long as you cite them properly. In subsequent chapters, we will suggest ways to make habits of good citation.

Common Knowledge

As we have written and will continue to discuss, you must cite all of the information that you find throughout the research process. This is what makes you an ethical and accountable researcher, essential qualities for building credibility with your audience.

However, what happens when, in your essay, you share information that everyone knows—facts, statistics, and stories that most people are familiar with? Should you cite those things, too? The answer can be tricky.

When you are including information in your research writing that is widely known and reported, that information could be considered *common knowledge.*

However, there are no clear boundaries or definitions for what can be considered common knowledge. And, while you wouldn't be expected to cite most of the information that qualifies as such, it is still important that you discern what is common knowledge and what is not.

You Do Not Need to Document It If . . .

- You are citing an encyclopedic piece of information that is easily verified, such as a well-known date, historical facts, birthplaces, and so on.

  Example: John F. Kennedy was assassinated on November 22, 1963.

- You are citing information that most of the general public *should* know.

    Example: There are three types of clouds: cumulus, cirrus, and stratus.
- You are citing information that has been well documented by numerous sources and that, therefore, has become general knowledge.

    Example: As of 2016, Michael Phelps, the Olympic swimmer, holds the record for the most Olympic gold medals.

However, if you are unsure whether an idea would be considered common knowledge, go ahead and cite the source. In the case of academic documentation, it is better to err on the side of too much rather than too little. Note cards, whether digital or hard copy, can help you keep track of these important citations.

The Art of the Note Card—Of Any Kind

Despite our general reliance on digital technologies for research, writing, record keeping, and any other host of conveniences, there are some tried-and-true methods that are delightfully low tech and might well remain so: the note card.

In fact, use of the note card can be one of a number of ways to help you avoid plagiarism.

Note cards allow you to do the following: you can summarize (rather than copy) content from your sources and accurately record in writing all aspects of the source that will readily allow you to compile your bibliography. You can create a paper note card or use the "notes" feature on your smartphone or tablet—and other, myriad possibilities. The point is to make whatever method you choose an organized one that gives you a way to record the information you need.

Therefore, while our ways of researching information have changed, our need to evaluate the suitability of a source and to document that source and cite it carefully *has not*.

Indeed, advice promulgated in 1972 by James McCrimmon in his celebrated textbook, *Writing with a Purpose* (Houghton-Mifflin, 1972), has fully transcended the test of time:

> When you begin intensive reading, you should also begin taking notes. The results of your preliminary reading may be carried in your head, but you are now beginning to collect the actual evidence from which your paper will be written, and it is important to the success of the rest of your work that both the form and the content of your notes be satisfactory. (232)

Always, and accurately, write the source on the card (or its equivalent) first; then, summarize the portion of the source that you are using, being careful to have just one such note per card or screen. If you are quoting an opinion, be sure to use quotation marks on the card, surrounding the quote, so that you remember to do the same in your paper. If you have been able to write a credible summary in your own words, you must still cite the source.

McCrimmon concisely and usefully summarizes his own recommendations regarding note taking; we therefore present them to you here, adapted with an occasional annotation in brackets to acknowledge that our ways of conducting research may have expanded and changed in recent years. The time-honored *criteria* for appropriate citation, however, have not changed, and they transcend the changes in our source materials and expanded ways of doing research. Remember, then, that we are using the word *card* expansively, denoting both its paper form and its digital equivalents:

- Put notes on cards (or individual screens, for instance, on your smartphone "notes" feature), not in notebooks [digital or paper], with one note to a card [or screen *so that you can organize and reorganize them as necessary when you craft your paper*].

- On each card identify the exact source of the note, including the page number [*if a book, or the URL or other appropriate ways to identify matter from digital sources*].
- Enclose in quotation marks the actual words of an author, whether the notes are statements of fact or of opinion.
- Summarize extensive quotations if possible, but still identify the source.
- Use direct quotation whenever the exact wording may be significant, especially if you are going to criticize a statement in the source.
- Be careful that your notes—whether direct quotations or summaries—do not distort the meaning when taken out of their original context. (McCrimmon 236)

Overall, then, keeping these points in mind, consider these tips for avoiding plagiarism:

Initiating Conversation

On your own or with a classmate, take a few moments to find an article from an online news source, a print newspaper, or a national magazine. Create "mock" note cards that are adequate enough for you to create a five-minute presentation to the rest of the class without your having to use the actual article/original source itself. How are you able to use keywords and author tags that effectively remind you of the piece's content and adequately credit the original source? As with the note cards you create for your actual research paper, make sure these practice tools do more than just repeat large quotes from the source; rather, your notes should be the results of your having summarized or put in your own words the information you want to convey. Remember that even information that is not directly quoted needs to be cited.

Tips for Avoiding Plagiarism

- Have an organized system for conducting your research, including note cards, keywords, and a working bibliography.
- Use your note cards to keep track of all bibliographical information that you will later need to cite your sources.
- "Recycle" the source language twice when paraphrasing: once for your notes and then again in your essay.
- Look at your notes—not the original source—when drafting your essay.
- Check your work against the original text to be sure you haven't accidentally plagiarized.
- Make use of good citation habits, including citing your sources as you write your rough draft. Do not wait until your draft is complete or then try to work backward, adding citations to text that is fully composed; you will make your work that much more difficult.
- When you've fallen behind on a project, don't be afraid to ask your instructor for an extension. (But be prepared for "no.")
- Read through your final draft and make sure that all necessary information is cited properly.
- Most important, give credit where credit is due!

To reiterate: using a system of note cards to track and organize your research—whether on a tablet, your smartphone, or on an index card—will make it easier for you to discern where the information came from and how you should document it appropriately in your essay. There are many note-taking applications for various electronic devices that will allow you to do what good researchers have always done: keep thorough and thoughtful notes. We encourage you to do whatever makes you feel the most comfortable. So, if you prefer hand writing your notes, then using a traditional index card may be helpful to you (this method has, after all, worked for decades).

If, however, you'd rather keep your notes on your electronic device (because, let's be honest, we all always have our smartphones or electronic tablets with us), then there are many ways for you to do that effectively.

Ideas Into Practice

As we have discussed, good note taking is the first step in avoiding plagiarism. It is also useful, front-end work, and it is a part of the research process that will help tremendously when you write your paper and create your bibliography. It is not only important that you keep track of all of your bibliographical information, but it is also essential that you keep a clear and precise record of whether the information you've written is directly quoted, paraphrased, or a product of our own ideas.

Regardless of the medium you choose for your note cards, consider modeling your notes after the ones in the illustration. When note taking, be sure to include the following: title of the source; author's name; page number; the information you want to remember; and, perhaps most important, whether the information is paraphrased, summarized, or directly quoted. Remember: Although it may seem cumbersome to do all of this note taking now, it will save you a lot of work once you begin writing and as you prepare your final draft.

Verse Reference

Author's Last Name

V.10   Nolland   p.875

Page Number

-reader comes with
positive look on
pharisees & negative
view on tax collectors

Paraphrase

Use this space to write your **note** from the source. Include only one major note per card.

Write if the note is a **summary**, **paraphrase**, or **quote**. This will help you correctly cite your sources when you write your paper.

CHAPTER four

Who Cares?
Identifying the
Problem

talking points

- What should I write about?
- How do I turn my big idea into a narrowed research topic?
- Why should I consider the audience when conceiving of a topic?
- Do I still need to have a thesis?
- What's the difference between a topic and an argument?

If you're reading this book, it is likely that you are in a writing class in which the instructor requires that you write a research essay. Your instructor has walked you through academic documentation, given you tours of the library and online resources, and has left you with three, perhaps terrifying, words: *choose a topic.*

Finding a Topic

Selecting a research topic is, for many students, one of the most daunting tasks in academic writing. It is also, as we tell our students, the single most important decision you'll make in the research writing process.

Not only will your decision determine whether your essay is received by an interested and invested audience, but it will also inform the scholarly work that you do for the next several weeks (and possibly for several months). You don't want to find yourself spending long nights in the library and online, researching something that doesn't interest you and that doesn't have an impact on those around you. Therefore, you need to choose your topic wisely.

If you are just starting your project, you will need to begin thinking through possible research topics that interest you.

Here are a few steps that you will consider in this chapter. We will ask that you:

First: Identify a list of subjects that interest you.

Next: Use *pre-searching* both to help you survey what resources are available to you and to help you further explore your broad interests.

Then: Focus your idea by narrowing your research subject into a workable, appropriate research topic.

Start with a Subject

It's perfectly acceptable to begin by thinking very broadly. In fact, the process of selecting a research topic can be represented visually as a funnel, such as the one you see in the illustration. You will start with a big idea and, through several processes that you'll read about in this chapter, you should be on your way to a narrowed and focused research question.

Provided that your instructor hasn't directed you to write about one topic in particular, your research subject can be inspired by a variety of factors, including both your personal interests and your favorite areas of study.

BROAD
SUBJECT   ....>

NARROWED
TOPIC   ....>

RESEARCH
QUESTION   ....>

To begin, compile a list of these broad subjects. Your list may look something like this:

Adoption
Rain forests
Fashion
Film
Music
Politics
Computers
Sports
World War II
Mahatma Gandhi

These subjects are not unlike topic headings that you would find in the library, and—as we've already mentioned—they can be general; don't be afraid to start big. These broad interests will serve as the umbrellas under which you will develop more narrowed topics and, eventually, a focused research question. Eventually, you will need to *argue a point of view* about your topic, one that you can prove with the resources available to you.

It is sometimes helpful to think about *conceptual* versus *practical* problems in research, as the conceptual problem, once the problem or topic is narrowed, is often more appropriate in humanities-related subjects than is the practical problem, more an appropriate scheme in scientific areas.

Initiating Conversation

Look at the list of broad subjects that we have provided on page **36**. Choose one, and with a group of your classmates or on your own, narrow down the topic to specific research topics within each of the following disciplinary contexts: for instance, under "film," in a nursing class, you might research educational films about communicable diseases; for a sociology class, those similar films might be a good resource for examining dating practices sixty years ago versus today; in a literature class, you might use films to compare the filmed versions of a play by Tennessee Williams and the text itself. Take another of the subjects (not film) and generate specific topics within different disciplines—for instance, music or politics.

Practical versus Conceptual Research Problems

Here's a *practical problem*: How do we improve the quality of drinking water in developing countries?

Certain disciplines lend themselves more readily to practical problems than others. For instance, many scientific problems pose a hypothesis, for which a solution is then found. Some scientific problems also lend themselves to quantitative data and analysis.

Here's a *conceptual problem*: Why did the Democrats win the White House in 1960?
The conceptual problem doesn't have a readily tangible result; the "solution" is often disputable, and therefore an appropriate argument—citing appropriate, relevant sources—must be made.

We are looking at a problem that lends itself to more qualitative research, leading to additional questions that will form the basis for research. So, for instance, you might ask the further question, "How did the first televised Presidential debate in 1960 change the outcome of the 1960 Presidential election?"

Pre-searching

When our students have first been assigned a research project and are beginning to think through possible topics of interest, we often encourage them to do a little digging before they finalize their research questions. This *pre-searching*, as we call it, usually involves conducting a few searches, both on the Internet and in library databases, using some of the broader subjects as keywords. These pre-searches serve two primary purposes.

First, especially when pre-searching library databases, you will be able to survey how many relevant resources—that is, resources that may be useful to you for your respective research topics—are available in your college or local library. The accessibility of applicable resources should be a factor when determining whether you have chosen the right topic. We always tell our students to set themselves up for success, and one of the ways to do this is to assure that the resources necessary for your project are readily available to you.

Consequently, you'll want to ask yourself several questions as you sift through your pre-search findings on several possible subjects:

How many books does my school library have about horror films?

Do I have access to any periodicals (journals, magazines, etc.) and other, credible online sources that may include articles about hiphop music?

What resources are available under the subject heading "child psychology?"

Finding answers to these questions now, and identifying valuable resources before you decide on your final research question, will streamline some of the work you will encounter throughout your research process. It might also save frustration down the line if you realize that several resources that you'd expected to find might not be available to you after all.

We also encourage our students to conduct pre-searches because, in addition to helping them survey available resources, these searches also help them to recognize and identify certain specific areas of interest within their subjects—something like "things I found on my way to looking up something else."

You may, for example, know that you'd like to research American snack foods for your project. Although that is a good start (and it illustrates that you are, indeed, thinking broadly to start), it is also a very large subject, and you will, ultimately, need to determine what point you will argue about snack foods. However, through some pre-searching—either by sifting through online articles or thumbing through the contents of a book—you may come to find a small facet of that subject that interests you. Perhaps you'll end up writing about how Twinkies changed in the face of World War II. Or perhaps you'll get caught up in the tale of the Wrigley chewing gum company and its influence on advertising.

Either way, the point is that pre-searching will likely lead to some information that you didn't know before or hadn't expected to find. And that information may lead you away from topics that have already been written about extensively and instead lead you toward a topic that is both new and interesting for you and your audience alike.

Moving from a Subject to a Topic

Once you have your list of subjects that interest you, it is time to begin narrowing them down to possible research topics. As we've already discussed, research subjects are usually broad and unfocused. They often take the shape of one-word terms or phrases: politics, sports, film, sports and the economy, and the like. Your topic, instead, should begin to identify what *aspect* of your subject is most interesting to you.

One of the best ways to begin this process of focusing is by listing those aspects that you find most intriguing. Go subject by subject and ask yourself, "What is it *about* politics or sports or film that I find so interesting?" This sort of brainstorming should push you beyond just identifying a general area of interest, and it should help you approach your research topic with much more specificity.

In addition, when moving from a subject of interest to a focused research topic, make use of the resources you find while pre-searching. When you begin exploring resources in the library, you will notice that the layers of depth within the library's database, in many ways, parallel the layers of depth you will be discovering throughout the process of developing a research topic. You begin with a broad subject, and these subjects are often very similar to the Library of Congress subject headings that we use to catalog texts.

For example, let's take a look at what we find in a library catalog when searching for sources on fashion. As you can see from the screenshot, that broad subject heading—"fashion"—is widely represented; there are over two hundred titles in this library that fall under this general subject.

However, you'll also see that there are several similar subject headings that may interest you, and these new subjects (fashion—Africa, fashion and architecture, fashion and art) may help you define further what exactly it is you would like to research for your essay. (And, clearly, even these somewhat more defined subjects are still very broad and will require that you further specify them.)

40

#	Number of Titles	Heading (Click to see titles.)	Heading Type
(See Also) 1	230	Fashion.	Library of Congress
2	2	Fashion.	General Heading
3	7	Fashion.	Sears list of subject headings
4	2	Fashion--20th century.	Library of Congress
5	1	Fashion--20th century--Exhibitions.	Library of Congress
6	13	Fashion 20th century History.	Library of Congress
7	4	Fashion--20th century--Pictorial works.	Library of Congress
8	1	Fashion--21st century.	Library of Congress
9	1	Fashion--21st century--Exhibitions.	Library of Congress
10	1	Fashion--21st century--Pictorial works.	Library of Congress
(See Also) 11	0	Fashion accessories	Library of Congress
(See Also) 12	0	Fashion Advertising	Library of Congress
13	3	Fashion--Africa.	Library of Congress
14	1	Fashion--Africa--20th century--Exhibitions.	Library of Congress
15	2	Fashion--Africa--Pictorial works.	Library of Congress
16	1	Fashion--Africa--Social aspects.	Library of Congress
17	1	Fashion--Africa, Sub-Saharan.	Library of Congress
18	1	Fashion and architecture.	Library of Congress
19	1	Fashion and architecture--History--21st century.	Library of Congress
20	23	Fashion and art.	Library of Congress

There are numerous Library of Congress subject headings for "fashion." Identifying the subject headings for the various subjects that interest you may help you identify a research topic.

If you click on the available titles for "fashion" and begin to survey the titles available, as we encourage you to do when you are pre-searching, you will start to see that the titles offer you keywords, topics, and ideas for your research paper.

Take a look at the screenshot, which shows some of the titles available in this particular library.

In just this preliminary investigation, we are presented with a variety of options for narrowing the initial subject. Perhaps you realize that you want to do research on fashion blogs or on one fashion blogger in particular and her or his influence on the fashion world. Or perhaps you'd like to talk about fashion jewelry and the new business models created by artisans on the East Coast. You can even be so specific as to choose a specific piece of clothing or accessory to research, focusing on the accessory's early history or development: how about *boutonnieres*?

#	Subject Heading	Full Title	Date	Format	Cover
☐ 1	Fashion.	Fashion design, referenced : a visual guide to the history, language & practice of fashion / Alicia Kennedy & Emily Banis Stoehrer with Jay Calderin.	2013	Book	
		Library Location: Main Collection — Call Number: 746.92 K35f		Status: Available	
☐ 2	Fashion.	Advanced style / Ari Seth Cohen ; foreword by Maira Kalman ; interview by Dita von Teese.	2012	Book	
		Library Location: Main Collection — Call Number: 746.92 C678a		Status: Available	
☐ 3	Fashion.	Ballgowns : British glamour since 1950 / Oriole Cullen, Sonnet Stanfill ; photographs by David Hughes.	2012	Book	
		Library Location: Main Collection — Call Number: 746.920941 C967b		Status: Available	
☐ 4	Fashion.	Europe : rising fashion designers / Patrick Gottelier.	2012	Book	
		Library Location: Main Collection — Call Number: 746.92094 G685e		Status: Available	
☐ 5	Fashion.	Meanings of dress.	2012	Book	
		Library Location: Reserve Collection 1st Floor Circulation Desk — Call Number: 391.0019 M483m 2012		Status: Available	
☐ 6	Fashion.	Sartorialist : closer / Scott Schuman.	2012	Book	
		Library Location: Main Collection — Call Number: 746.92 S392s 2012		Status: Available	
☐ 7	Fashion.	Steal her style : fashion icons and how to get their look / Sarah Kennedy.	2012	Book	
		Library Location: Main Collection — Call Number: 746.92 K36s		Status: Available	

Just as there are numerous subject headings for "fashion," there are also numerous titles listed under each subject heading. These titles can also help you narrow your focus.

It can also be just as helpful to take a careful look inside the books that you find when trying to identify a topic for your research. If you would like to write about Mahatma Gandhi, for example, but are having a difficult time figuring out exactly what *about* him you would like to research, try inspecting the table of contents in a book to find a topic that interests you. *The Essential Gandhi: An Anthology of His Writing on His Life, Work, and Ideas* (Vintage Press, 2002), for instance, includes the following chapters in its second edition:

Civil Disobedience Succeeds
Gandhi's Road to Jail
Victory in South Africa
Segregation in India

Sex, Sanitation, and Segregation
Gandhi's Advice to Negroes
Gandhi on Socialism and Communism

If you see a chapter title that interests you, perhaps one of those listed, read the chapter more thoroughly and decide whether you would like to let one of these more specific subjects inform your research topic. Indexes are also good places to look, as the headings provided there will inspire many of the same ideas as will the table of contents.

Using Questions to Refine Your Topics

Once you have created a list of possible research topics, it is time to start working through your list to find the best option for your essay: what aspect of this topic can be argued appropriately within the span of the paper? How many resources and what kinds will I need to be able to make this argument effectively? Because research is often about inquiry, you can begin this process by raising these and additional questions about the topics in your list. These questions should push you to further define what *exactly* you want to say about the topics you have identified.

What kinds of questions should you ask? Well, that depends. You'll have a sense of whether you're asking the right questions once you have a workable topic and argument for your research paper. It's probably best to avoid the kinds of questions that lead to "yes" or "no" answers; rather, you're looking for questions whose answers speak to particular aspects of the topic.

Here are a few possibilities. Although we can't provide you with an exact formula—a formula in this instance won't be helpful anyway—we can model for you several possibilities that you can adapt to suit your own work.

Let's look at aspects of this process together, using the examples we've cited earlier in the chapter.

Using journalistic questions can help set boundaries for your topic: Who? When? Where? What? Why?

For example:

GENERAL SUBJECT:	FASHION
Who?	Women
When?	1960s
Where?	America
What?	Miniskirts
Why?	To express and empower

Possible Research Question

How did the miniskirt reflect not only the cultural movements of the 1960s but also the economic boom of that era?

Is your research aimed at a particular audience—in addition to the instructor?

If so, what might that audience want to know? For instance, are you writing to an advanced, highly expert group of film critics when you write about scary movies, or are you writing for a general, somewhat educated audience?

Possible Research Question for an Informed Audience

How do the cinematic techniques of Brian De Palma, particularly mise-en-scène and cross-cutting, parallel and pay homage to selected films of Alfred Hitchcock?

Another Example

How did aspects of Hitchcock's *Psycho* influence the films of Brian De Palma?

Possible Research Question for a General Audience

How well do scary movies fare at the box office, and how does their economic performance often defy the reviews published by critics?

Ask yourself what you think the audience might already know.
What is common knowledge about the subject, and what might be aspects of the subject that you can bring to light? Consider the very large topic of World War II. Ask yourself, then, "What are things that the general public already knows about this subject? What's worth writing about?"

Things people know (or should know) about World War II: Japanese bombing of Pearl Harbor in 1941; Axis Powers (Germany, Italy, Japan); Key Figures or Issues (Franklin D. Roosevelt, Winston Churchill, Adolf Hitler and Nazism).

Things people may not know (and you may come across these in pre-searching): Gender roles switching, with men away at war and women out of the home and at work and in factories; specific effects of pivotal battles; the oppression and murder of Jews, Gypsies, and homosexuals in Germany and elsewhere; Italian participation in the war; the days leading up to Pearl Harbor; the time after the European war had been won—but before the war in the Pacific was resolved.

However, there are aspects of the general knowledge topics that could—and should—be investigated as possibilities for research, as "general knowledge" sometimes refers to knowledge that merely scratches the surface of an issue. The point is that you should be aware of what your audience knows and what you might contribute to advancing the reader's awareness and knowledge of a subject.

Possible Research Question (or, in this case, topic)
Although many students learn in high school about the Holocaust, many might not be aware of attempts on the part of Jews to escape Germany on transports designed for both adults and children—some with success, some not—and the complicity of the United States in foiling one particular rescue attempt.

The subjects we've provided as an example here are, of course, just examples, and they are likely less than relevant to the work you need to do. The point, however, is this: the possibilities for research topics are boundless, and the challenge remains to narrow a topic and find a focus for your research efforts.

That is, it is essential to focus your thinking and move toward a research topic that is specific enough so that you can explore it within the time allowed and pages required for your essay. And, as we often tell our students, the more specific and manageable the topic is, the easier it will be to successfully write your research paper.

We encourage you to keep pushing for a narrower and more focused topic, continuously asking yourself the following:

- Does my topic still seem too broad?
- Could I do sufficient research on this subject within the time constraint of my assignment?
- Do I feel that I know where to begin my work, or do I feel overwhelmed by all of the information available on this topic? If so, how might I begin to sort through this information?

The answers to these questions should help you identify whether you are ready to move forward with the research process.

Turning Personal Interests into Appropriate Research Topics

Often, when talking with students who are struggling to find something to write about, we find that they have overlooked something central: their personal experiences. Although it is important to distinguish between personal writing and argument-focused, academic writing, it is also important that you begin to develop the capability to analyze your own interests and experiences in ways that are reflective of critical thinking.

Don't underestimate your own ability to turn your personal experiences into appropriate research topics. Consider your personal interests, your cultural heritage, and social issues that affect you and those around you. Any of these could lead to viable research topics—topics in which you will be particularly invested!

SAMPLE STUDENT RESEARCH TOPICS—SOME IN DISCIPLINES, SOME INTERDISCIPLINARY

Sciences:	Increased Instances of Flooding Due to the Increase of Impermeable Land in Urban Centers. The Effects of Glacial Deterioration on Small Coastal Habitats in Alaska The Impact of Over-Fishing on New England Ecology Do Local, Midwest Honey Farmers Replenish the Bee Population? Are Paleo and Keto Diets Nutritionally Sound? California's Emissions Testing and the Battle against Climate Change
Humanities: Literature, History, Popular Culture, Art History	Women in the Work of Aimé Césaire Taylor Swift and the Theme of Retribution Weegie and the Realism of Street Photography The Evolution of the Chicago Teachers' Union The Rise of Tobacco and the American Plantation Lyndon Baines Johnson and Civil Rights Legislation Economics and *Their Eyes Were Watching God* *Uncle Tom's Cabin* and the End of Slavery Picasso and Political Propaganda Gordon Parks and the Democratizing of Photography
Social Sciences:	The Deteriorating Safety Net for America's Poor Nuclear Nonproliferation in the Twentieth Century The Myth of the Absentee Father in Contemporary Television Drama Early-Twentieth-Century Immigration Policies Stereotypes of [Name a Group] in Social Media (or Television or Film) Immigration Policy Then and Now

Finding Significance and Identifying an Audience

One of the most important aspects of writing your research essay will be identifying and assessing your audience. For most students new to the research process, the concept of an audience can be a little confusing. Who is your primary audience, anyway? Are you writing this essay for your instructor? What about your classmates? Should you anticipate that a larger academic community will receive your work?

The truth is, it can be tricky to negotiate through these answers as a student writer. Although you likely cannot expect for your work to be read by academics in the larger field of study, you do need to imagine an audience larger than just your instructor and your peers.

You see, writing a research essay is, in some ways, similar to having a conversation. The scope of your research will be greatly informed by whom you imagine having this conversation *with*—and the ways in which it is most appropriate to address that particular audience. For instance, is your audience highly educated? A good friend who's smart but who knows nothing of your subject? Experts in the field?

Think about the following questions:

- To whom am I writing?
- Who stands to benefit from the research I am doing?

- How can I ensure that my audience is interested in my topic? How can I further define my essay's purpose to further pique their interest?
- How much can I assume my audience already knows about my topic?
- How can I demonstrate my authority on the subject?

The style, tone, and diction of your writing will be affected by these answers. You must determine who your audience is, and then you must find an approach best suited to that particular audience.

Diction and Tone

In addition to what you have read in Chapter 2, it is important to consider diction and tone. Your choice of language and your tone will (or should) have everything to do with assessing your audience appropriately and then understanding how best to address that audience.

For instance, here is a situation that emphasizes the importance of choosing your words (diction) carefully: if you are asked by your parent to wake up your young sibling—who has recently done something to annoy you—your choice of words and tone will likely differ than if your parent has asked you to wake up your kind (and generous) visiting aunt or uncle. And it's not unusual for us to have to code-switch (that is, change our language and word choice as would be right for a particular situation) from word choices and tone that are appropriately used among our friends to language and tone that are appropriately used in school or on the job.

Although "CU LTR" might work well for a text message to friends and family, it likely will not work well in writing an academic paper where highly refined conventions apply. (It likely isn't the best way to text a supervisor or instructor, either.) Keep in mind the need to address your possibly complex audiences appropriately when you are writing.

Crafting a Thesis or Posing a Research Question

Once you have decided on a topic, you must begin mapping out your game plan for the rest of your research and the best way to argue your point of view. Usually, it is best to begin this process by articulating your topic as either a thesis statement or a research question. This statement or question—whichever best suits your particular focus—will be the guiding idea for the direction of your essay. Therefore, it is important that you identify what you will argue as soon as you are ready to begin your work. (And, of course, remember that "argument" in this context doesn't mean something combative; rather, it is a statement of what you expect to prove in your paper, a helpful guide for your reader—as well as for you.)

A thesis statement is something of a signpost. It condenses your essay's argument or intention into one or two sentences that usually, although not always, will appear within the first few paragraphs of your essay. The thesis will help you organize your ideas, and—if done correctly—it will help provide your reader with a signpost that explains what the essay will be about, what information you are trying to relay, and what argument you will be making. In most instances, a strong thesis statement is an expected and highly significant component of a successful research paper. The absence of a thesis statement, or a poorly crafted one, can signify a lack of focus on the part of the writer.

A successful thesis statement will do the following:

- Give direction and focus to an essay or research paper. This direction assists both the writer (by serving as a tool for planning and organizing the essay) and the readers (by serving as a road map for the paper).
- Provide claims that will be backed by evidence throughout the body of the essay. Thesis statements are not statements of fact; you must support your assertions with accountable and credible research.

- Be narrow and concise. Remember, the scope of the essay's focus must fit the amount of time available to research and the number of pages required in the assignment. Again, don't confuse yourself and, ultimately, your readers, by announcing too broad a thesis.
- Engage your readers and allow them to see the purpose of your research.
- Preempt the possibility of your reader surveying your thesis statement and asking, "So what?" because of its clear purpose.

  Some Examples
  Miniskirts are signs of empowerment. (Ineffective) The writer has not written a thesis that can be readily proved by evidence because the statement is too broad. Whose empowerment? The fashion industry? People wearing the miniskirt?

Are miniskirts appealing to men? (Ineffective) The writer has written a thesis statement that isn't a thesis statement—anything with a possible "yes" or "no" answer is not something that can be argued in a research paper.

Although popular lore seems to indicate that women's hemlines rise and fall with the economy, recent history proves that fashion trends stem from far more complex economic contexts. (BETTER) This is a more restricted thesis statement and will be followed by another statement that indicates how the writer plans to prove his or her argument—indicating what are, in fact, the more complex economic contexts that will be explained.

Of course, although it is best to begin your research process by reviewing the sources you've gathered and then crafting a thesis statement, the statement itself should remain flexible until you have finished your essay. Throughout the research process, you may, and undoubtedly will, find new evidence that leads to a revision of your initial argument and that helps you reshape it.

The Difference between a Topic (or General Subject) and an Argument

To reiterate: Your *thesis* allows you to effectively *argue a point of view regarding your subject*, as the differences among the following will illustrate. Note how the writer narrows down the general subject toward an effective thesis that argues a point of view:

Topic/General Subject:	Pollution
Type of Pollution That Interests Me:	Water
Cause of This Pollution:	Oil Spills
Specific Example That Interests Me:	The BP Gulf Oil Spill

This particular student is interested in the effects of the oil spill on gulf beach resorts—in this instance, because the student grew up in this region, and family members' business interests were affected by the disaster. After studying and analyzing a wide range of sources on the economic impact of the Gulf Oil Spill, the student narrows the topic still further to analyze the economic comeback of the gulf region and develops the following working thesis/argument:

> *Although British Petroleum has committed funds and other resources to the redevelopment of affected resorts in the Gulf region, the efficacy of these efforts remains under dispute.*

> *The rebuilding of Gulf Coast tourism is the result not only of the passage of time, but also of strategic efforts and partnerships among industry, small business owners, and marketers.*

What is effective about this thesis statement and the argument it puts forth? The precise meaning of the arguments is very clear. In the first, for instance, the writer has promised to explain the nature of the dispute and the arguments for and against the effectiveness of the efforts made by the oil company to rectify a difficult situation. It is also strongly suggested that the writer will provide just enough context for the intelligent reader so that the reader has a basis for judging the arguments.

Here is another example of a complex thesis within a paragraph that points to the writer's argument. The student, Nadezh Mayo, writes about "Sexuality, Race, and Class in the Court Case *Rhinelander v. Rhinelander*"[1]:

> This particular case seems to have disappeared from popular accounts of history. It was not a Supreme Court case and it is

---

[1] The full text of Ms. Mayo's research paper appears in the Appendix.

53

not as well known as other cases pertaining to racial restrictions on marriage (in fact, only two lawyers are known to have access to the full court transcripts [Onwuachi-Willig, 2401]). For example, many people have heard of the case *Loving v. Virginia*, in which an interracial couple from Virginia fought for the right to be together in 1967 and won, legalizing interracial marriage throughout the United States. The case of *Rhinelander v. Rhinelander* may not be as well known, but the trial is an equally important snapshot in American history. The court proceedings express American conceptions of race in the 1920s, as well as American ideas about the roles of men, women, and sexual boundaries in the context of race. To describe the trial as an attack on interracial marriage and the "pollution" of the white race by blacks is not wrong, but it is incomplete. Upon closer examination, the court case *Rhinelander v. Rhinelander*, although fought on the grounds of racial fraud, in fact has as much to do with sexuality and gender as it does with race. Indeed, it is nearly impossible to think about the *Rhinelander* case without addressing the important interactions of race, sexuality, and class in public perceptions of Alice—a poor, black woman.

As Mayo's purpose is complex, her thesis is not neatly boiled down into one, simple sentence; rather, it takes several well-crafted sentences to make clear what she will argue.

Ideas Into Practice

As we have discussed in this chapter, developing a research question involves working through a series of steps, beginning with identifying broad subjects that interest you. Use the chart we have provided here as a guide to help you keep track of your topic ideas and to organize the notes you collect during the pre-searching process. Keep in mind that research itself is somewhat recursive. That is, you likely will find yourself doing the types of evaluation of sources that we suggest in the following chapter as you gather the resources you need to help you focus your paper—as we delineated in this chapter.

General Subject:

Pre-searching Notes:

What Interests You Most:

Narrowed Topic:

Thesis or Research Question:

CHAPTER five

The Wikipedia Problem: Evaluating and Trusting Sources in a Digital Age

talking points

● Why is it important that I find credible resources?

● In an online context, how do I discern what is "real" from what is "fake?"

● What makes a resource reliable?

● How can I evaluate resources?

● Why do I have to go to the library when I have Google?

● You mean I can't get all of my information from Wikipedia?

Although it may seem a long time ago to some, it was in 1998 that Google's search engine went live. Not that long afterwards, in 2001, Wikipedia debuted as the first online collaborative encyclopedia. Although we are quick to think of both of these Internet start-ups as cultural boons, it's also important to consider the ways that both Google and Wikipedia have in some ways been a detriment to our intellectual lives.

Quick Fact

"Google" was first used as a verb in 1998—the same year the site debuted. It was added to the *Oxford English Dictionary* in 2006.

Research in a Digital Age
Digital Information: A Detriment or a Boon?

Most likely, you don't remember a time when you couldn't quickly find the answers to all of your questions through an Internet search. You've been part of a world where you can access an inordinate amount of information without having to consult anything in hard copy, much less a book. In many ways, you're part of a population that has more easy access to more information than ever before.

Is this a good thing? Well, that depends. Having more information than one can process argues for careful analysis and evaluation of these sources. And that need seems more acute now than ever. We've only begun realizing how this accessibility—this "instant answer culture"— has changed the ways that many students engage in academic practices. In particular, the way you conduct research and the way you think about research have inarguably been altered by these digital worlds.

But some things don't change: that is, good research takes time, and, although information may be easier to access in a digital era, the scholarly processes necessary to produce credible and valuable academic writing haven't changed much at all. In fact, the ability to discern the quality and appropriateness of information is more necessary than ever.

So, while we as professors want our students to develop a technological literacy that enables them to make use of the wealth of digital content available to them, we also want students to understand the importance of honoring a long-standing tradition of scholarly research, one that transcends the medium (digital, book, etc.) holding the information you need.

However, among any concern about the need for the enhanced ability to sift through information, there's additional good news. You are more technologically savvy than any other generation. And, as much as we want you to be able to thoughtfully navigate your way through this sea of information, the truth remains: In many ways, that access presents endless possibilities for scholarly research and academic engagement—but with many resulting challenges. You have opportunities and readily accessible information in ways that were unforeseen even a few years ago; we want to help you assess and use these in as savvy and in as critically a way as possible.

Scuba Diving versus Jet Skiing

To reiterate: In 2008, *The Atlantic* published Nicholas Carr's "Is Google Making Us Stupid?" in which the author argues that our frequent use of the Internet is causing physiological changes to our brains. Clearly, this potentially has great impact on the way we read and engage with texts. The piece seemed to strike a chord, quickly becoming popular. In explaining how his own reading habits and abilities have altered noticeably, Carr notes, "Once I was a scuba diver in the sea of words. Now I zip along the surface like a guy on a jet ski."

We have seen this metaphor play out in the way many students engage—or in the way they *aren't* engaging—with sources in their academic writing. More and more, students are doing the kind of skimming Carr alludes to in his article. Students pull quotes from sources to satisfy a minimum number of resources in the bibliography, and they aren't thoroughly evaluating and reading the sources from which they are quoting. Do you recognize yourself here?

We want you to be mindful of this phenomenon when conducting your research: the ways frequent Internet use may have an impact on your ability to engage with and fully understand and analyze texts. Constantly ask yourself, "Am I scuba diving or am I jet skiing?"

Misinformation and "Fake News"

Why does the information in this book matter to our lives outside of the classroom—indeed, outside of a college education? In Chapter 1, we introduced the term "information literacy." But part of being literate about information is being savvy; it requires your being careful about which information you trust and which information you allow to influence you and your choices.

Of course, in terms of a research essay, what this means is that you must—as we reiterate throughout this book—choose sources that are authoritative and factual, as your ethos and the effectiveness of your argument depend on them. However, in our lives as citizens, understanding how to weigh claims made by others—whether it's your uncle during a dinnertime argument or a news organization or an organization that purports to be a news organization—is equally, if not more, important.

You have undoubtedly heard the term "fake news," and while the manipulation of information is not at all new, the Internet has exacerbated its promulgation and has more than unduly influenced our perceptions of situations, people, and world events. That is, although news outlets, artists, satirists, and the like have long been accused of misleading the public, our communal and frequent engagement (obsession?) with the Internet on a regular basis has made us far more susceptible to untruths and unbalanced news reporting that appeal to fear or extreme positions and biases than ever before.

Further, Internet searching engines and social media platforms are actually developed to feed into our individual biases. In fact, online search engine algorithms and social media feed our biases by showing us "news"—articles, images, and so on—that are based on things that we have searched for in the past. As little as thirty years ago, while there were always newspapers and magazines that fed these biases, they were not "delivered," so to speak, in the immediate ways that they are now through our devices. Most people in those years, which also preceded twenty-four-hour cable news networks such as CNN, MSNBC, and Fox, would watch a standard news program in the early evening with trusted news anchors and reasonably balanced rather than slanted information about what had happened during the day. Most of us were exposed to varied points of view, even if our own views were strongly held.

Additionally, because the Internet is rife with misinformation and algorithms that prey on our personal biases, it's easy to find articles that confirm what we believe or fear, regardless of whether that information is grounded in fact. This is called *confirmation bias*. We have all been guilty of skimming through our social media accounts, seeing a "news headline" that aligns with a preconceived notion or that merely attracts our attention in a way it had not before, and "liking" it or sharing it without doing our due diligence about its veracity. This has been a problem for such platforms as *Facebook*, which, arguing that it is not a media outlet, chose not to vet posted articles and headlines, many of which have been proven to be false and inflammatory but which have influenced issues of public policy, and, unfortunately, our electoral process. As a result of all this, we have become conditioned to reject or be uncomfortable with any information that challenges us or that doesn't validate what we already believe or want to believe. This is a regrettable sea change in the way we receive and perceive information.

Therefore, what are credible sources—for instance, for news? Or for information about the Paleo diet? Or for advice about what stocks to invest in? And why does it matter, not only for the research essay you are writing, but also for your life? At the end of this section, we ask you to consider various ways to evaluate sources and establish their credibility—even if they do not agree with your personal views.

More and more, our students are proposing research questions to which they believe they already know the answer. Just as some turn to nightly opinion shows to validate positions that they already hold, others similarly choose research questions that reflect personally held assumptions that they do not even consider might merit a challenge. You might ask yourself, "Am I genuinely curious about this research process?" Are you entering this research process to learn about and make a credible argument, or are you expecting merely to affirm your position on a particular topic—and restricting yourself to resources, credible or not, that underscore your own position?

Evaluating Sources
Why Do I Need to Trust Sources, Anyway?

Trustworthy sources, and your acknowledgment of those sources, contribute to your being a trustworthy writer. No matter the source or topic, an expectation among writers—academic or otherwise—is that you are accountable; that is, that you can be counted on as a writer who has done the often painstaking homework of finding the right information to back up your point of view. Remember, these factors can go a long way toward demonstrating your ethos as a research writer.

It is generally expected that you are arguing a point fairly and accurately, that you are arguing it in your own words, and that you have consulted appropriate sources that back up your argument. Equally important is that you have acknowledged those sources as having contributed to your own work. Just as good writing takes time, so, too, does finding and analyzing the right sources for your work—as does using them appropriately.

Stop and Consider

If you have an electronic device with you—and your instructor thinks it's a good idea—look through your social media accounts. If you are among those who eschew Facebook, Twitter, and the like, team up with a classmate who participates in one of these platforms.

With any one of these, evaluate any bias in what you read, viewing it through the lens of what we've just discussed about confirmation bias, fake news, and misinformation. How did you determine bias? Why are you sure? Do you notice any trends? Do the headlines and articles on your social media feeds lead you in any particular direction? Do they tend toward one particular perspective? (And is that because you joined particular groups to see/hear only that perspective?) To what emotion do certain headlines appeal? (Fear? Guilt?)

How do our social media circles—whom we follow, our friends, whom we like—limit the lens through which we see the world? Why is this a problem? How can we prevent this?

Easier Isn't Always Better

All that said, the heading for this section, and what follows, might seem obvious: Not all resources are created equal. That is, one of your primary tasks as a researcher is to determine which resources are reliable and which are not so that you can craft an accountable, well-defended argument. But this task was considerably easier before the Internet came along. Before the availability of search engines and online databases, researchers relied on card catalogs and large machines displaying microfiche copies of newspapers and other types of printed, archived materials. The smart researcher-writer spent hours perusing library bookshelves, reading through potential resources, and thumbing through printed indexes, often waiting weeks for books through interlibrary loan services. (And despite the Internet, the latter is still true.)

Although digitalized searches have made it easier for researchers to find and fully use such resources, the Internet has also made it more difficult to discern whether those sources are dependable, as virtually anyone can create and launch a website and make it seem authoritative. To reiterate, here's the thing about websites: anybody can have one. The Internet has made it possible for large amounts of often unfiltered information to be shared in an effortless fashion; it has also made it possible for people to "publish" their work—work that, oftentimes, hasn't been reviewed or fact-checked by anyone, much less a responsible and reputable editor. It's true that you can access scholarly databases, government reports, and other valuable resources online, but you have to be savvy in the way you search for and decide to use these sources.

Think about your recent Internet searches. If, for example, you are using the keywords "fast food" to search for resources to use in an essay about America's obesity epidemic, you are as likely to stumble upon a website entitled *Bob's Burger Adventures* as you are to find a comprehensive study of fast food nutrition from the United States Government.

It is likely that the first source in the Google list will be a sponsored source, not necessarily one that's appropriate for your research project. Perhaps the first link is the result of a concerted effort by the site's owner or author to "game" the Google system and ensure that the site appears as a top link. (You are likely aware that the top links aren't necessarily the most authoritative sources on a given topic—and yet they might be. It's up to you to determine this.) As a researcher, then, know that it is your job to evaluate whether these sources meet your needs and meet the standards of the academic communities in which you are participating—and those for whom you are often writing.

Whereas the Internet presents a wide variety of information with an equally unpredictable range of quality and reliability, libraries (apart from access to the Internet in library buildings) present a different set of opportunities. In a library, you are surrounded by texts and materials that have—in one way or another—been vetted. That is, books have gone through long and tedious publication processes involving initial review by a potential publisher, reviews by other scholars in the field, and rounds of revision—and all this before publication. Then, many books will have been reviewed in significant journals after publication. Similarly, magazine and newspaper articles have often been fact-checked by multiple staffers, and scholarly publications in most journals also have been peer reviewed.

So, while the Internet certainly does house valuable information, it is necessary that you hold Web-based resources particularly accountable for the same level of credibility that you would find—perhaps more easily and reliably—on library shelves.

The Good News: Using Wikipedia and Google Effectively

Despite what we have said about how the Internet requires us to be more discerning researchers, the truth remains that at some point in the process, most researchers will use the Web. It is in acknowledging these realities—and acknowledging the ways in which our intellectual lives now often inhabit digital spaces—that we want to find a happy medium. That is, just as we would not encourage you to do all of your research on Wikipedia or Google, we also do not want to discourage you from approaching these valuable resources in smart and savvy ways.

The truth is that both Wikipedia and Google *can* be valuable tools during the research process. Of course, you likely use these websites to conduct your own casual "research" every single day. You Google reviews of the Thai restaurants in your area. You look up movie times. You find a reliable hair stylist. You quickly scan the Wikipedia entry about a famous philosopher that a friend mentioned in passing. We all do these things; we are all conducting some form of research—using these online tools—regularly.

When it comes to academic research, however, it is necessary that we approach these Web resources differently. Let's discuss some ways of doing that.

Google

Google, as we discussed earlier in the chapter, is one of the world's most popular search engines. As you already know, using Google gives you access to more information than could ever be quantified. That said, the results you get in Google are completely dependent on the way you execute your search—and on the ways in which you evaluate the results for their usefulness and credibility. Later on in this book, we will talk about using effective keywords and Boolean phrases that will assist your search. However, there are steps you can take, even before you enter your keywords, to ensure that you are targeting your search to yield the most credible and appropriate results.

There are two tips that are especially helpful. The first is to try your searches using Google Scholar. Executing a search on Google is like asking the engine to rummage through a series of a million drawers, looking for anything—reviews, photographs, websites—that has the keywords you typed into the search bar. Using Google Scholar (scholar.google.com), then, is like telling the search engine to look only in drawers containing academic sources. That is, when you do a search using Google Scholar, all of your results should come from reputable scholarly publications. So you are much more likely to find the kind of information you will need for your research projects.

Another way to refine the search is to limit the results to websites ending in .edu, .org, or .gov. These domains—the websites ending with these suffixes—are much more likely to provide researchers with high-quality information than are many websites ending in .com or .net. You can refine your searches in this way by accessing the "Advanced Settings" on your Google homepage.

Wikipedia

Just as you can approach Google searches in a sophisticated way, there are also ways that you can use Wikipedia to your advantage. Although most academic researchers likely would not use Wikipedia articles in their work, as they are user created and not always fact-checked, many Wikipedia entries now contain something that can be very valuable during the research process: a bibliography.

If you scroll to the bottom of nearly any entry on Wikipedia, you will find a list of sources—and many of those lists include hyperlinks. This means several things: not only are the authors of the various Wikipedia entries telling you where they found the information they used to write the article, but they are also, in many cases, linking you directly to that information somewhere else on the Internet. So, while you wouldn't want to use Wikipedia as an exclusive resource in your own work, you can use Wikipedia to find other resources—many that would, after you examine them, be considered valuable and credible. This kind of "bibliographical diving," as we like to call it, can be extremely fruitful, leading to a trail of resources—many of which might have their own bibliographies, too!

Therefore, there are myriad ways to use the Internet's limitless collection of resources to your advantage. Remember that you have control over how you navigate this sea of information, that you are responsible for determining the validity of that information, and that there are ways to ensure that what you find along the way will be useful to you as you begin doing your own writing.

Although we speak specifically about Google and Wikipedia because of their preeminence as this book is written, the larger point here is independent of the particular resource that you are using. No matter what source you use, approach it with thought and careful analysis, intellectual qualities that transcend the medium or the website.

Initiating Conversation

Although they often make for good reading, entries on Wikipedia aren't always accurate. However, they can be useful resources for bibliographic material. Find a Wikipedia entry about an historical figure or event that interests you and follow the "digital paper trail"; that is, scroll to the bottom of the entry and explore the various articles, books, and the like that are cited. Although you likely will not use the Wikipedia entry itself for your own bibliography, which of the other resources seem to be useful for a research paper on the particular topic you have chosen? What makes them effective?

Determining Appropriate Resources

Before you can begin assessing the credibility of resources, you first need to determine what kinds of resources will be the most useful to you. What kind of essay are you writing? What is the topic? And—more important—what is the purpose of your essay? Do you want to share new information? Present an opinion? Make an informed argument? Does your information need to be qualitative or quantitative or both? (See Table 5.1.)

Answering these questions before you begin looking for resources will help your search stay goal oriented. Knowing what kind of resources you *don't* need can be as useful as knowing what kind of resources you do need.

Table 5.1   TYPES OF DATA

As you move forward with your research, what kinds of data will best help you support your arguments?

QUALITATIVE DATA	QUANTITATIVE DATA
Qualitative (quality) data are based on observation, description, and other immeasurable information.	Quantitative (quantity) data deal with numbers, statistics, and information that can be measured.

Scholarly versus Popular Sources

Chances are (again, depending on your topic) that you will likely make use of both scholarly and popular resources. Scholarly resources, such as research-based books and articles published in academic journals, are often written for an audience of faculty members—that is, scholars and researchers. These include publications such as *African Studies Quarterly*, *Journal of Religious and Popular Culture*, and *The American Journal of Medicine*. As we mentioned earlier, most scholarly resources have been through a peer-review process. Most often, they will also include citations, footnotes, and a bibliography.

Popular resources, on the other hand, are written for a more general audience. Many of these are the kinds of publications you would find while standing in line at the grocery store. However, it is important to understand that credibility varies even among popular resources. *Time* magazine and *Newsweek*, for instance, are both very reputable newsmagazines, with credible reporters and commentators.

However, magazines such as *Us Weekly* and *People*—while culturally relevant—are not nearly as likely to offer the kind of reliable information you need when writing academically, unless, of course, your assignment is a critical analysis of these types of publications. Even then, however, you will likely seek other reviewers and critics of popular culture as you delineate your arguments and work to support them.

The Art of Skimming

Having just maligned the scuba diving/jet ski simile, we do, nonetheless, encourage you to learn the art of looking through various sets of materials thoroughly, effectively—and yet efficiently. This is where appropriate skimming—as opposed to the shallow knowledge that Nicholas Carr warns against—can be useful, especially when you first begin reviewing materials. It will be necessary to learn ways to judge fairly quickly whether a source will be worth your careful perusal and study. This is when you might want to use strategies known as "pre-reading," such as looking carefully at the table of contents; looking carefully at the index; the overall structure of longer books and articles; and, for academic articles, taking time to study the abstract rather than the entire piece (at least at the start).

Learning to "read" these various components of (especially) longer sources can assist in your sorting through overwhelming amounts of materials in a responsible way. For instance, in a collection of articles and longer texts, your review might result in your using only one chapter out of, say, twenty. Don't discount longer volumes or texts as you evaluate resources; parts of a source might prove to be very useful to you later on. Cultivating the art of skimming, or, one might say, "selective looking," might help.

Evaluating All Sources

Although you need to be especially careful when looking for resources on the Internet, you should also be asking yourself a series of questions that test the reliability of any resource you find—whether online or in print. These questions can help you begin to analyze and screen sources and determine their credibility—and, ultimately, their usefulness to you and to your work.

Some Questions to Ask When Evaluating Resources
What do you know about the author?

For most of the types of writing that you will do at a college or university, it is important that you know as much as possible about the person who authored your source. In scholarly publications, for instance, you will always see both the author's name and the author's academic affiliation. Is the author associated with a university or professional organization? What is the author's educational background? Is the author considered an expert in his or her field? Is the author in any way self-interested, or trying to sell something, that might undermine his or her credibility? The more you know about the person that created the text, the more you can trust that the text will be a reliable resource for your research.

At the same time, however, you may want to determine and analyze what others in the field think about a particular author. For instance, someone with what appear to be good academic credentials might, for instance (and in an especially extreme example), prove to be a denier of historical fact.

Is the source backed by a reputable publisher?

With printed texts and materials, it is usually easy to determine who published a given work. You can find this information on the copyright page or the spine of a book. Who, then, is the publisher? Have you heard of this publishing company before? What other work has it published? University presses are usually highly regarded, and the books they publish have undergone an especially rigorous process of evaluation.

Of course, just as someone can publish his or her own website and make it seem authoritative, writers can also self-publish their own books through corporations that take otherwise unpublishable manuscripts (by most standards) and publish them for a price, usually paid for by the author. So, although a printed text may seem reliable, it may not have been vetted by reviewers or editors before being allowed into print.

The point? Be judicious when evaluating all resources—even hard-copy books—so that sources on which you rely to bolster or to advance your argument are credible. To a great extent, your own credibility as a writer depends on these choices.

Again, the issue of credibility is exacerbated with online sources. With online sources, you must also make sure that information is sponsored by a well-known university or organization—that it has been evaluated appropriately. Much as you can look at the copyright page in a book for information, you can also look at the URL of an online source. Web addresses that end in .gov and .edu, for instance, can *generally* be trusted.

Has the source been peer reviewed?

As we have noted, most published academic writing—whether an article or a book—has gone through a peer-review process. Through peer review, experts in the respective field read through and respond to written scholarship or the results of research. For that piece of writing to be published, these peer reviewers will have first acknowledged that the author has made a credible and significant contribution to the field.

You will find that comparatively few popular magazines, newspapers, or online resources have been through similar review processes, and, depending on the topic and the purpose of your own writing, you will want to use the latter type of source very carefully and wisely.

Is the source current? Does it need to be?

There are times when it is important to look at older, often archival, research as a way to make your point and support your argument. As always, these considerations will depend on your topic and the purpose of your writing. For instance, in an argument one of us advanced regarding scholarly work in a particular field, it was important to look at articles in journals dating from the mid-1950s to illustrate that many of our contemporary concerns are not, in fact, new. If you are a history major writing a senior thesis on the Civil War (and depending on your topic), you might also choose to dig into documents and sources from the time of that conflict. A literature major might also find that documents related to popular culture or reviews at the time a particular work was written will be useful for his or her analysis of, say, a previously ignored novel.

Yet for many writing assignments, however, you must be aware that information is always changing and—if the topic demands it and you want your academic writing to be relevant and timely—you need to make sure that your resources are also contemporary. What is the publication date? Is there a newer edition of a particular source? Are there more contemporary voices that you should consult? Part of your analytical and decision-making process as you select the sources to support your writing might be to determine whether your resources are current, and if they are older, to understand why you have made a careful and deliberate choice to use them. Is it a seminal work in the field? Have there been critiques of the book, but critiques that do not dispute the basic premise—or, depending on your topic, sources that legitimately dispute the basic premise of an older work?

Does the source provide bibliographical data?

In most instances, you will be required to create a bibliography when writing a research paper. It is important that you are able to communicate—through citations and footnotes—where you found the information you have chosen to use as support for your argument. So it makes sense that the best kinds of resources are often the ones that are equally accountable for where their information came from, too. Look for sources that have bibliographies so that you can analyze what types of work the author used to support the central arguments of the article or book.

Has this source been cited by other writers?

One of the best ways to tell whether you can trust a source is by figuring out whether other scholars have read and trusted that same source as well. You can use databases, such as the *MLA International Bibliography*, to see whether other scholars have cited the source that you are considering using in your own work. And even Google offers opportunities to research how often a scholarly article has been cited by other scholars.

All that said, be aware, though, that there are many articles that—for one reason or another—never quite catch on in the scholarly world but that are equally worthy of your consideration as you research your subject and topic. Sometimes you might find a highly credible scholarly gem that others have missed. Such are the pleasures and challenges of being an accountable researcher and writer.

Is the argument reasonable?

Although the degree to which a resource is being reasonable is highly subjective, trust that you are savvy enough to know whether a source is being fair and trustworthy. Most reputable scholars will do their best to present all sides of an argument, and they will not intentionally present a biased point of view. Be wary of sources that seem aggressively opinionated and one sided—again, depending on your topic.

CARS: Credibility, Accuracy, Reasonableness, Support

Using CARS is an effective tool to use for evaluating resources. This set of criteria will help you as you assess the quality of the sources you find (see Table 5.2).

No matter how masterful we may be as writers, we are only as good as the evidence we use to advance our arguments. As an intellectual thinker, your ability to find, analyze, and best use appropriate sources enhances your accountability and your ethos as a communicator.

Table 5.2   CARS

The Cars rubric is yet another way to determine the quality of your information.

Credibility	Trustworthy source, author identified, can be contacted, known or respected authority, author's credentials, evidence of quality control, organizational support.
Accuracy	Current, date of update/revision, factual, detailed, exact, comprehensive, audience and purpose reflect intentions of completeness and accuracy, gives the whole truth.
Reasonableness	Fair, balanced, objective, reasoned, no conflict of interest, absence of fallacies or slanted tone. Is the information likely, possible, or probable?
Support	Listed sources, contact information, available corroboration, claims supported, documentation supplied. A source you can triangulate (find at least two other sources that support it).

*Source: http://nurseweb.ucsf.edu/www/a1_p4v2.html.

Ideas Into Practice

The checklist below is to help you capture what is sometimes the "randomness" of finding good sources—in other words, "things I found as I was looking for something else." We suggest that you make a few copies of this checklist and keep it with you as you begin your research. Try using the comments section to document any information or ideas you may have about the sources you find. Keeping organized notes throughout the research process will also help to better organize your ideas once you begin writing.

Evaluating Resources ➤ A Checklist

The Source
Title:_____
Print or Web Resource:_____
Author:_____
Publisher:_____
Publication Date:_____

Author and Authority

Is the author credible?	Yes No Don't Know
Comment:_____

Is the source backed by a reputable publisher?	Yes No Don't Know
Comment: _____

Has the source been peer reviewed?	Yes No Don't Know
Comment: _____

Does the source have a bibliography?	Yes No Don't Know
Comment: _____

Response and Reason

Has the author's work been well received by peers?	Yes No Don't Know
Comment: _____

Has this source been cited by other reputable scholars?	Yes No Don't Know
Comment: _____

Does the author's argument seem fair and balanced?	Yes No Don't Know

CHAPTER six

What Counts and Why? Finding and Engaging Sources

talking points

- How do I find resources?
- What's the difference between a search engine and an online database?
- How do I navigate all of the resources in the library?
- Do keywords make a difference in search results?
- What's the difference between a primary and secondary resource— and why does it matter?

At this point, you should have a narrowed research topic in mind. Although you have probably done a bit of pre-searching (as we encouraged in Chapter 4), it's likely that you have yet to find all of the resources that you will use to write your essay. In this chapter, we will help you begin that process.

Finding Resources

Of course, the best way to begin to find resources is to first identify the kinds of resources that you will need. To start, think about what your instructor has asked of you. Do you have to have a specific number of resources or types of resources that you must find? Are online sources acceptable? Have you been discouraged from using any type of encyclopedia? Do your sources have to be peer reviewed—that is, with information published only after other professionals in the field have vetted it first? Take stock of your "must haves" and let them guide you through your research process.

You also need to think about your research topic and your essay's audience—both of which should inform the kinds of resources that you think will best support your argument. Does the nature of your argument lend itself to more popular resources—for instance, blogs and magazines? Or does your research question demand reputable and vetted sources, such as scholarly articles? The answers to questions such as these will influence the direction your research should take. Spend a little time developing a game plan before you hit the stacks, both virtual and brick and mortar.

Here are some basic research tips to help you get started:

Document Everything

In a previous chapter, we talked about the importance of note taking. It is imperative that you keep track of information as you find it. You may find an article or a book now and decide that you don't want to use it, only to later find that it might have helped you. (And no matter how good your memory, it is best to assume that you won't remember that terrific source later on without writing it down or making a record of it in some other fashion.)

So start a working bibliography on day one, using note cards, the notes feature on your smartphone, a tablet, or a website (easybib.com, for example) to easily track the titles and authors of the sources as you find them. As you keep track of everything you find, you then have notes to direct you later in the research process, with your options for which sources to use at the maximum. And keep in mind that most online databases will also give you the option to e-mail yourself a link to the full article so that you can consult it later.

Collect Now, Sort Later

The first few days spent researching can prove to be overwhelming. Depending on your topic, you will likely encounter an endless trail of resources—many more than you could ever reasonably use. Don't get bogged down with heavy reading just yet. It's perfectly acceptable to amass a pretty sizable collection of books, articles, and other materials that may—or may not—prove to be useful. Evaluate the resources quickly and efficiently (using the criteria we gave you in Chapter 5), and then plan to thumb through them more thoroughly later on. Again, having options is the key.

Don't Limit Yourself

Yes, you will probably be able to find some interesting and relevant books in your school's library. However, you may also be able to find appropriate resources elsewhere: in a database of newspaper articles, in a scholarly journal, or even on a webcast. The point is this: the more avenues you exhaust, the more likely you are to find a diverse and varied array of resources that can, and will, add to your credibility as a researcher and provide options for the way you ultimately "slant" your argument and your work.

Knowing the Difference: Primary, Secondary, and Tertiary Sources

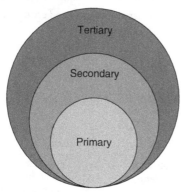

Although your sources are of various types, they are all interconnected.

As a researcher, you will likely be relying on a variety of sources to help you construct your argument. During the research process, you will come across three different types of resources: primary, secondary, and tertiary (see Table 6.1).

Primary sources are original materials. They are often firsthand accounts written or recorded by an eyewitness and may also contain raw data. Primary sources are "pure," without interpretation, and they have not been changed. Some examples of primary sources include photographs, patents, speeches, audio recordings of events, interviews, diaries, physical artifacts (fossils, historical clothing, etc.), letters, and legal documents (birth certificate, marriage license, trial transcripts).

Secondary sources are more difficult to define. They are often created with the use of primary sources, and they may be the result of someone having evaluated and interpreted raw data. So, while a primary source may be considered evidence, a secondary source is the result of reviewing and discussing that evidence. Some examples of secondary sources include biographies, scholarly writing (peer-reviewed articles and journals), reviews and critiques, dictionaries, and most magazine and newspaper articles.

Table 6.1   EXAMPLES OF PRIMARY, SECONDARY, AND TERTIARY SOURCES

TOPIC	PRIMARY	SECONDARY	TERTIARY
Horror films	Hitchcock's *The Birds*	Scholarly critics writing about the film; reviews of the film	*Encyclopedia of American Horror Films*
The civil rights movement	Transcripts of speeches by Martin Luther King, Jr.	Biography of Martin Luther King, Jr.	Wikipedia blurb about the civil rights movement
Fine art	Painting by Frida Kahlo	Review of painting by a reputable art critic	ArtStor database

Tertiary sources present a list or collection of primary and secondary sources. These sources are often seen as a guide to primary and secondary resources, as tertiary sources are presented as an overview. Keep in mind that most instructors (and those who adhere to their subject area conventions) will frown on tertiary sources as part of your bibliography—unless, of course, you're doing a study, say, of Wikipedia itself. Some examples of tertiary sources include manuals, indexes, databases, bibliographies, most textbooks, and encyclopedias.

Finding Sources Online

Many, if not most, of the preliminary searches you will conduct as you begin the research process will take place on the Internet. Online search engines and databases are all readily accessible and are integral tools throughout your research process. However, knowing how to navigate these online tools efficiently and accurately can determine whether the results will help you with your research writing or confuse you even further.

This is why (and as we discussed in Chapter 5, "The Wikipedia Problem") it is extremely important that you are able to evaluate and filter the information that you come across when using the Internet to find sources. Again, you have read a good deal about this in Chapter 5, and it is important that you keep the tips we gave you in mind—tips for conducting research in a digital age and for evaluating the resources you find. Use these tips to help you refine your evaluation skills.

Online Library Databases versus Internet Search Engines

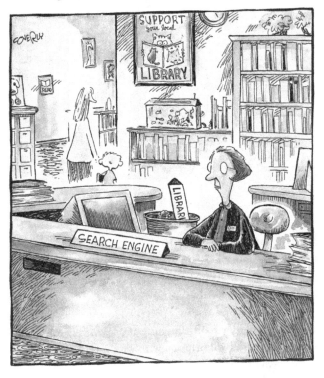

When conducting research online, you can consult both your library's online database and more popular Internet search engines, such as Google and Yahoo.

The *online databases* for your school or local library provide access to sources that are, for the most part, more credible than others a researcher might find. Most libraries subscribe to a variety of academic and discipline-specific databases, giving you access to scholarly articles, newspapers, and magazines. So, when you search the library's database, the results will be limited to materials that have likely appeared in print and have previously gone through an editorial process.

Library databases, such as EBSCO, Academic Search Premier, JSTOR, and InfoTrac, are not often free and available to the public. You pay for access to these resources with your tuition dollars, and your school libraries will select databases that best serve the programs and classes that their respective institutions offer, increasing the likelihood that the resources you find through library databases will apply to the kinds of research you are asked to do in your class.

On the other hand, *Internet search engines*, as we've discussed earlier, provide access to a sea of information (or, depending on what you find, misinformation). Unlike library databases, however, the Internet has no gatekeeper. There aren't necessarily any librarians carefully selecting which resources should be available to you, any editors overseeing the various stages of publication, or any academics vetting and peer-reviewing the information you find.

So, whereas your database searches will almost certainly lead you to information that is organized and reliable, the information you find on the Internet will vary significantly in terms of quality. (Remember our earlier reference to *"Bob's Burger Adventures"*?) When using search engines, you have to be the most discerning about which sources are appropriate and which are not.

Initiating Conversation

At this point, you likely have a working research topic (or at least a general subject) in mind. Using both an online search engine (such as Google) and a library database (such as EBSCO), search for

(continued)

resources about your topic using the same keywords or phrases for both tools. Compare the differences. Discuss your findings with a classmate and summarize them for discussion with the class. What, overall, are the differences in your searches? How does the information differ? What are the overlaps?

All of this doesn't mean, of course, that these search engines can't provide you with useful resources. You just have to be savvy in your approach to both the language you use to conduct the search and the results provided (see Table 6.2).

Table 6.2   TOOLS FOR ONLINE RESEARCH

Although both search engines and library databases can be useful to researchers, there are marked differences between the two.

SEARCH ENGINES	DATABASES
Free to the public	Paid for by your library
No gatekeeper	Content has been reviewed by librarians
Information is not always reliable	Resources have been through an editorial process
Information is disorganized	Information is organized by experts

Choosing Your Keywords Carefully

Whether using an online database or an Internet search engine, the keywords you use to execute your search will determine the quality of results that are returned to you.

Quick Fact
The Library of Congress, which was established in 1800, consisted of 740 books and three maps. Today, the library houses more than 32 million titles and is the largest book collection in North America.

A library database is nothing like Google. Although it is acceptable to type in "scary movies" in Google, there are certain protocols for using library databases. For instance, the Library of Congress database archives resources about movies under the subject heading "film." So, if you type in "movies," you may not get the results that you want or need.

How can you get to know these keywords? The online "call page" for every resource will list not only the author and the title for each source, but it will also give the Library of Congress subject heading. Once you have identified one source that fits the scope of your project, you can then look to the call page for that source and find the subject heading that will lead you to further sources—because you have found the correct "keyword." However, even though Google sources might seem more forgiving, as you will always receive *some* type of result when you attempt to search through Google, you must still be very discriminating about what it is that you find.

Let's say, for example, that you want to do research on the overconsumption of fast food in America—a topic we have used as an example before. Your first instinct may be to open up Google and search for "McDonald's." Why not? McDonald's is the most popular fast food restaurant in the country, right? However, this search is likely to turn up a vast and overwhelming diverse network of information: addresses for the McDonald's nearest to you, nutritional information for the Big Mac and the double cheeseburger, photographs of hamburger packaging, reviews of local McDonald's restaurants, and so forth. Because there is so much information—often too much—identifying which information is appropriate and reliable can be a difficult and somewhat daunting task.

Instead, when you are conducting searches through any search engine, we encourage you to think carefully about the keywords or terms you use for your search. Here is another way to think about it:

the larger the network of information you are tapping into, the more carefully you need to choose the keywords that you use to increase the likelihood that you will find what you're looking for.

Although popular search engine results are not vetted or restricted by any particular parameters, the situation is different for your library's online databases, such as EBSCO, Academic Search Premiere, and so on, which are primarily limited to magazines, scholarly journals, and newspaper articles.

Let's take a look at the difference.

Here are the results when we search for "McDonald's" using Google's search engine:

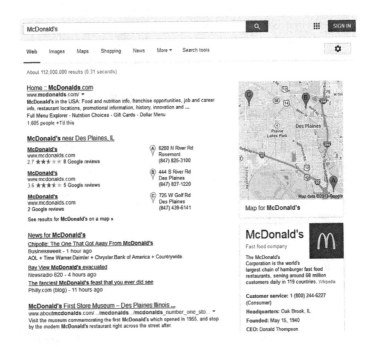

And here is what we get when we search for "McDonald's" as a keyword using EBSCO:

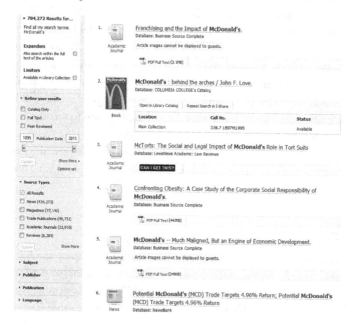

As you can see, the results vary enormously, and you need to target carefully the type of results you want. However, if neither of these yields the specific kind of information you seek, you will need to rethink your strategy. In other words, these search results serve as a good indication that your keyword or keywords need to be refined.

Boolean Searches

Boolean searches use the connecting words (called operators) "and," "or," or "not" to make your search phrases more specific. Using this type of phrasing when searching either popular Internet websites or library databases can help yield results that are more appropriate to your topic.

For example, searching for "McDonald's and obesity" will be much more fruitful to you than simply typing in "McDonald's."

In addition, Boolean searches limit the results to fit more specifically with the scope of your search. If you just searched for "video games," for example, you will likely get thousands of results. If you search for "video games and violence," however, your results will be significantly refined, leaving you hundreds of options to sort through instead of thousands.

So, as we have mentioned many times in this chapter, the keywords you use to execute a search will most certainly determine how useful the results will be.

Finding Sources in the Library

Although your first instinct might be to run to your laptop and begin searching for resources using your favorite search engine, we urge you to first make use of your college and local libraries. Remember what we've said before: libraries host collections of sources that have already been vetted, for the most part. Your chances of finding credible and reliable sources in your school library are much higher than your chances of finding them independently on the Internet.

Consequently, do resist the urge to do all of your research from the comfort of your own desk chair. And remember the pleasures of finding things that you happened to run across on your way to looking for something else. Although this can happen online, it can also happen as you scan shelves of books or look through old microfiche screens.

Getting to know your library—and your library's online catalog—is half of the battle. And, luckily, some of that type of work actually *can* be done from your desk chair. Nearly all libraries, especially those associated with colleges and universities, have websites that are easily navigated.

For example, let's look at the library homepage for each of our institutions:

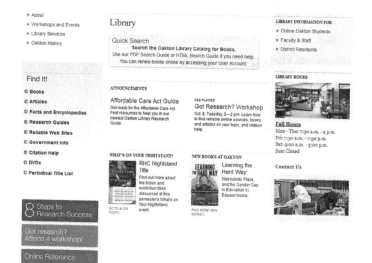

This is the library homepage for Oakton Community College. What information seems most important? What are similarities and differences with the pages at your own college

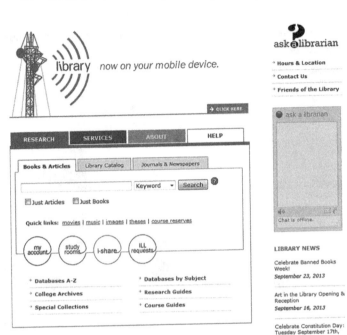

And this is the library home page for Columbia College Chicago.
What information seems most important? What are similarities and
differences with the pages at your own college?

Although the graphics, design, and layout among institutional
websites may be significantly different, you will notice, however, that
both websites offer similar options to students. Most notably, the
homepages for both libraries provide immediate access to their online
catalogs and databases.

Most likely, the homepage for your library will look very similar,
and it will be useful for you to compare yours with these to see differences, similarities, and whether ways to find different types of information vary from institution to institution. As you look at these
pages and investigate those at your institution, you will also have the

option to search for a variety of texts, including books, articles, and multimedia materials.

Using Online Catalogs to Find Books

Your library's online catalog will help you search for books housed within the library by a variety of criteria: subject, author, keywords, title, and so forth. The catalog's chief function is to assist you in identifying the books that best meet the criteria you specified and then to direct you to where those books are located within the library.

As you can see, the first half of your work can be done online, but you may find that you will have to venture into the library to complete your search—and, we trust, that you will benefit from scanning shelves of books that might well turn up other possibilities for your work.

Find Books

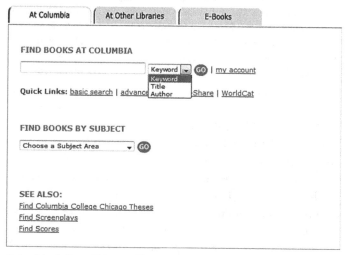

Columbia College Chicago. Most online card catalogs will resemble this one.

As you'll see in the graphics provided, the library homepages for both Oakton Community College and Columbia College Chicago provide students with quick and easy access to the card catalog. Look for the "Books" or "Library Catalog" link, and there is where you will begin your search.

Because you likely have some experience navigating library catalogs, we are not going to walk through the step-by-step process of initiating these searches. Once you've found any number of books, articles, and the like—and once these are recorded in writing or some other way of documenting the source information (yes, even phone photos of the title page of a book and its call number and other relevant information)—what if your topic merits other types of research methodologies?

Stop and Consider

One of the joys of using the library—seriously—is finding books that you hadn't expected to find as you look for the one you'd found in the online catalog. If your library has stacks, do a little shelf-snooping at books located close to the one you're actually looking for. What else have you found? How might it enrich your research? What did you find or learn on your way to looking for something else?

Interviewing and Field Research: Generating Your Primary Data

You may find yourself involved in a research project—perhaps, say, in anthropology or oral history, to name just two—that will require you to interview or observe others. Volumes have been written on the art of the interview, for instance, and clearly, there will be examples of best practices online. You might also need to conduct a survey; you may find you need to generate field notes. But how do you know you are approaching these other types of information gathering in the best way possible? What follows is a very brief overview of some fairly complex forms of information gathering.

Here are some tips for generating the raw data that you will incorporate with other sources. For field notes, jottings, or observations that are collected at a specific site that is relevant to your research topic:

- Try to refrain from participating in the activities you are there to record; this will allow you to take the role of the observer and researcher.
- Write as much as you can while you are at the site and save for later your "weeding" of what was important and what wasn't.
- Consider all of your senses: what you hear, smell, and see.
- Remember that it can be as important to record your reactions to what you see as it is to record what you see. Be mindful of your own responses, but remember to keep observing and recording.

For interviews, the art of engaging with someone else or others to record their thoughts and observations on a particular subject with which they likely are familiar:

- Enter the interview informed. Know something about the person you're talking with and be sure you have context regarding the subject about which you're interviewing.
- Have a script of informed questions that allow you to stay focused and on point.
- When appropriate, go off script to help your subject be comfortable; ask follow-up questions that might lead to something revelatory or new about your subject.
- Avoid double-barreled or leading questions that seem to entrap or force a certain kind of response from your interviewee. Open-ended questions will actually allow you to get the kind of response you need.
- Be skeptical of your technology. Assume that your recording device will fail and have a backup—even if that backup also includes a pad and pencil.

Remember that if you do a very good and thorough job, your interview material may well become fodder for additional presentations or research opportunities.

For survey research, the opportunity to ask short, simple questions of potentially large audiences:

- Know your audience and choose the form of dissemination best likely to reach them.
- Develop questions that require short answers and that will encourage your audience to take the time to respond.
- Consider using free, online survey tools (such as Survey Monkey) as a way to reach particular audiences, keeping in mind that for some types of audiences, you may need to send hard copy to ensure access.
- Allow yourself enough time to collect multiple responses with survey research; you want to make sure you have plenty of lead time before your deadline.

These forms of data gathering will complement other materials and resources that you find—even more traditional sources such as books. The following activity will assist as you determine what types of sources and data you might need.

Ideas Into Practice

What kinds of sources do you need? It depends on the discipline and your subject, but here are some possibilities.

Different disciplines expect different kinds of sources and even expect certain types of conventions in writing that may differ from others' expectations. For instance, scholars in literary studies more often than not use the present tense when discussing an author's work, as the *work itself still exists* (as in "Charles Dickens says . . ."). Historians, on the other hand, more often than not will use the past tense (as in

"Presidential historian Max Beschloss said . . ."). We will remind you of these examples again later on.

As researchers make sense of the sources they have, categorize yours according to the conventions of your subject as primary or secondary sources. This is just a partial list, and you might consider creating the equivalent of a spreadsheet to record and question the relevance of the various sources you have thus far:

Anthropology: Recordings; films; scholarly articles and books (secondary); first-person narratives and documents; qualitative data.
My source:
Relevance:

Literary Studies: The primary subject itself (the novel, poem, story, etc.); scholarly articles (secondary); author manuscripts and letters; and possibly, reviews written at the time the work was published.
My source:
Relevance:

History: Scholarly books and articles; narratives, documentation of witness accounts.
My source:
Relevance:

The Sciences: Laboratory reports; data in a variety of quantitative forms (graphs, tables, etc.); data from one's own laboratory work and/or survey results.
My source:
Relevance:

CHAPTER seven

Yours, Mine, or Ours? Integrating Resources

talking points

- I've done all of my research. Now what?

- How can I use both my own ideas and those from my resources?

- How do I summarize?

- How do I paraphrase (without plagiarizing)?

- When should I use a direct quotation?

- What is "patchwriting" and how can I avoid it?

You have chosen a research topic, you have spent a lot of time conducting research and collecting resources, and now it is time to answer the next big question: How do you use all of the information you have? That is, how do you integrate the resources you have found into your own research writing?

From Research to Writing

In this chapter, we will help you explore the various ways in which you can incorporate research material into your own work—your paper. Namely, we will discuss the ins and outs of summarizing, paraphrasing, and direct quotation—the primary skills you will need when engaging resources.

Beginning the Conversation

As we have mentioned, writing a research essay is not unlike having a conversation with others—in this case, your academic peers. Many ideas—many voices—come together in your work. Therefore, as with any conversation, one of your primary tasks must be to recognize when you should enter the conversation and when you should let others do the talking.

Ultimately, as the research writer, it is your job to shape the conversation; you develop the framework within which everyone else's ideas (your resources) are contained. We often tell our students that this kind of balancing act can sometimes lead to a bit of tug-of-war within the writing. It is very easy for research writers, especially beginning research writers, to lose control of their essays; they let the resources take over.

As you read this chapter, however, it is very important to remember that your research writing must depend on your own words and ideas. You are not simply a patchwriter, quilting together the ideas of others (something we will talk more about a little later). You are responsible for conceiving of and constructing your own argument, and you will need to make use of the resources you've collected to help *support*—not *create*—that argument.

Let's talk about how to begin.

Integrating Resources: Summarizing, Paraphrasing, and Quoting

Summarizing

You are likely already familiar with how to summarize. This is one of the first skills we learn as we are taught to engage with texts and to recount our understanding of what we've read. That is, at some point when you were in school, you were undoubtedly asked to read a book. And, to hold you accountable for having done that reading, a teacher probably asked you to tell the class what the book was about. You were asked for a summary.

We summarize the resources we use to construct our own research arguments for much the same reason. Just as your teacher needed to make sure that you read and understood your assignment for class, your essay's audience needs to make sure that you read and understood the resources you have chosen to include in your paper—and that you have employed them appropriately.

A good summary—the kind of summary necessary for academic writing—shows that the researcher has a firm grasp on and is able to readily identify what is important in a resource. It shows that you, as an accountable, smart writer, can read, understand, and then synthesize resource material to the benefit of your own essay and the argument you want to advance.

Stop and Consider

Stop writing and start talking. Often, the best way to figure out whether you understand a source or actually find it useful for your purposes is to talk about it out loud with someone else. Go ahead: team up with a classmate. Choose a source from your working bibliography, perhaps one that is particularly perplexing to you, and

> talk about it and how you think it is useful to you. See if you have difficulty either explaining what it means—and ask your classmate to look at the source, too—or connecting it to your own argument. (If your colleague agrees, you might want to record these conversations on your smartphone to provide fodder for your work.)

Paraphrasing

To paraphrase is to communicate the ideas in a resource, using your own language. Much like summarizing, paraphrasing, when done well, shows the audience that you are able to clearly and accurately explain what you have read in a resource without relying too excessively on direct quotation.

Furthermore, paraphrasing can help the researcher to contextualize and support an argument. It allows the writer to offer overviews of the source material without surrendering control of the essay to another scholarly voice (or a set of scholarly voices). In addition, paraphrasing can keep your paper from appearing to be merely a set of connected quotations with no contribution of your own ideas—and without these attributed, summarized ideas.

However, it is in their attempts to paraphrase that we see many of our students verge dangerously close to plagiarism. Often student writers struggle with making their own paraphrased sentences differ enough from the original text in a satisfactory way.

When a reader can spot overlaps in language and/or sentence structure between your essay and the original source, it can hurt your credibility (and your ethos) as the researcher. These sorts of similarities, which students often claim are unintentional and which sometimes actually are unintentional, can be mistaken for plagiarism.

For example, let's look at the following passage, which reproduces our earlier paragraph:

> When a reader can spot overlaps in language and/or sentence structure between your essay and the original source, it can hurt your credibility as the researcher. These sorts of similarities, which students often claim are unintentional and which sometimes actually are unintentional, can be mistaken for plagiarism.

The following attempt at paraphrasing actually plagiarizes the original text:

> Readers can spot overlaps in language and/or sentence structure when they look at your essay and the original, and it can hurt your credibility. Even if you claim that this is unintentional, it can be mistaken for plagiarism.

This next paraphrase verges on plagiarism:

> Students often unintentionally plagiarize when attempting to paraphrase a resource. Readers can easily spot this kind of plagiarism by finding overlaps between your essay the original source (Holdstein and Aquiline 101).

Although this writer has cited the source, the attempt to paraphrase isn't careful enough, and the writer would do well to use a direct quotation. And this final attempt, which does not plagiarize, successfully paraphrases the original text:

> As Holdstein and Aquiline warn, one of the ways students can ensure that they are not plagiarizing the original source is to paraphrase very carefully. Students should move beyond simply rearranging words or changing sentence structure and make sincere attempts to communicate the ideas of the original source without relying on the same language—unless they are using direct quotes.

If your language looks too much like the language of the original, the reader can often tell, and students may be accused of plagiarism (Holdstein and Aquiline 101).

Direct Quotation (Quoting)

When you use the exact language of a source, and you include that language in your essay verbatim, you are quoting. Direct quotes are usually easy to spot in an essay, as they are surrounded by quotation marks as an indication that the words and ideas are taken from a research source and did not come from the research writer him or herself.

When students first begin writing the results of their research, they tend to rely very heavily on direct quotation. This seems to be the case, primarily, because student writers have difficulty establishing and owning their own voices—something we discuss at the beginning of this book. (However, we know that it is sometimes also an attempt to increase page length.)

Therefore, we encourage our students to use direct quotes sparingly, suggesting that they only quote a source directly if the original phrasing is integral to the overall idea or points they are trying to make. Similarly, only use a direct quote when the language in the source is as important as the idea being communicated.

Avoid Patchwriting

Being highly selective of how and when you choose to incorporate direct quotations will help you avoid *patchwriting*. Patchwriting—sometimes referred to as quilting—occurs when the writer relies too heavily on resources, excluding his or her own ideas and analysis. What results is something akin to a quilt of quotes devoid of any sort of thesis, analysis, or synthesis from the writer. Again, it is important to remember that you are using quotations from sources to support *your* argument; your essay cannot be composed of only source material.

Use the Quote Sandwich

One of the best ways to avoid patchwriting—and one of the best methods for using quotes in your essay—is to learn to make a *quote sandwich*. Rather than including a quotation in your essay with little or no analysis or explanation, make sure to sandwich each quote with your own words and ideas. Your top "piece of bread" should include a few lines introducing the relevance of the quote and providing any contextualization. Your bottom "piece of bread" should include a few sentences explaining and analyzing the quotation. For example:

> In their book, *Who Says: A Writer's Research*, Holdstein and Aquiline emphasize the importance of avoiding patchwriting, suggesting that research writers should "make sure to sandwich each quote with [his or her] own words or ideas" (Holdstein and Aquiline 85). Using a quote sandwich can help researchers maintain control of their writing, assuring that they use text from resources as a way to support and not replace an argument.

In this example, you can see that the direct quote is *sandwiched* between sentences that introduce and explain the quote. In addition to the quote sandwich, you might also find it helpful to remember the acronym ICE: introduce the quote (using the signal phrases we discuss next), cite the quote, and then explain the quote in your own words. Remembering to use quote sandwiches—or the ICE method—will ensure that you are properly contextualizing the words from your sources within your own argument, using your own language.

Using Signal Phrases

A *signal phrase* is a word or group of words that introduce a piece of information from a text or a direct quotation.

It is important that you use signal phrases regularly, because they will let your audience know when you are integrating material from one of your resources and when you are engaging with the ideas of other scholars. Using these phrases regularly will help keep you accountable and honest.

We encourage you to not only use signal phrases but also to experiment with the language you use is these phrases. Resist the urge to rely on the same old signal words again and again (e.g., "Jane Smith says").

While there are many to choose from, and we encourage you to create your own list of verbs to use in signal phrases, here are a few to help you get started: admits, agrees, argues, asks, believes, calls, claims, comments, confirms, defines, denies, declares, echoes, emphasizes, estimates, finds, illustrates, implies, mentions, notes, predicts, proposes, reasons, recognizes, refutes, responds, reveals, states, suggests, tells, thinks, warns, writes.

Summarizing, Paraphrasing, and Direct Quotation: Knowing Which to Use and When

When is it appropriate to summarize, paraphrase, and quote directly?

It's best to paraphrase and summarize when the wording in the original source seems less important than the ideas or meaning of that source. Using both of these techniques will allow you to maintain your own voice in the paper and a kind of rhetorical consistency—that is, the approach to the argument as determined by the way you have established the sound and feel of the paper rather than the voice of the experts you're quoting.

Another benefit of summarizing and paraphrasing is that they will allow you to provide an overview of extensive and complex sources that may be essential to your argument but whose details are less important for the reader to know.

On the other hand, as we have mentioned, choose to quote directly when the wording of the original source is as important as the meaning. When the original text communicates a complex or significant idea—or if the passage is a particularly famous one, if not common knowledge—and if accuracy is especially important, then be sure to quote the passage directly. Quotes of one to three sentences in length should remain in the body of the paper, whereas longer quotes should be made into "block quotes" set apart from the body of the paper. Block quotes are often formatted differently, depending on your citation style. So be sure to check for the particular conventions of the style within which you are working.

Table 7.1 charts the ideas articulated in this chapter in a succinct format that you will find useful as a checklist.

Think of integrating sources as entering into a complex set of conversations—or better yet, think of yourself as the symphony conductor who is also playing the piano. Find a way to enter this conversation by acknowledging others' contributions that have brought you to your own argument; as the pianist-conductor, you're integrating and acknowledging others' contributions to the whole while engaging in your own contributions to the conversation as well.

Table 7.1   OPTIONS FOR INTEGRATING AND SYNTHETHIZING OTHERS' IDEAS

METHOD	HOW DO I DO IT?
Summarizing	• Briefly explain the main ideas, key concepts, and arguments found in a source. • Strive for concision. Only include what is necessary for your own essay and your argument. • Read the source thoroughly to assure that your summary is both accurate and ethical. • Include a citation that identifies the source of the information you have summarized. • Make sure to clearly differentiate between your own ideas and the ideas from your resource.
Paraphrasing	• Reword or rephrase the information in a source, communicating the source's ideas using your own language. • Make sure to complete the translation, avoiding any overlaps in wording or sentence structure with the original source. • Read the source thoroughly to assure that your paraphrase is both accurate and ethical. • Include a citation that identifies the source of the information you have paraphrased. • Make sure to clearly differentiate between your own ideas and the ideas from your resource.
Quoting	• Use the exact words from a source, making sure to use quotation marks appropriately. • Be very selective about how and when you choose to directly quote a resource, only doing so when the exact language from the source is integral to the meaning. • Make sure to sandwich each quotation with your own explanation and analysis. • Avoid taking a quote out of context. Make sure that you accurately represent the original author's intent. • Include a citation that identifies the source of the quotation.

Initiating Conversation

If you have a series of notes or note cards on your topic, challenge yourself to write a small part of what might eventually be your completed paper without relying on direct quotations. This will exercise your ability to adequately summarize and paraphrase the material. Afterward, discuss with others the challenges you face in having to refrain from quoting your original sources—or, if quoting is inescapable, how you have limited your use of direct quotes while citing appropriately your paraphrases or summaries. Then, reflect on how your own thinking and writing processes differed when you had to craft your own well-supported arguments—without using directly the words of others.

Ideas Into Practice

Select a key resource that you've identified in your working bibliography. The length of the source doesn't matter; for this activity, if you select a longer book, for instance, you will have determined which section of a longer piece is useful to you.

After carefully reading and annotating this source, communicate the main ideas of the passage in three separate ways, using the methods we've suggested in these pages:

> *Paraphrase* the portion of text you have selected; then
> *Summarize* the portion of text you have selected; then
> *Directly quote* aspects of text you have selected.

This activity might seem a bit redundant; however, it will illustrate how you should use these various techniques appropriately when integrating ideas and source materials. By comparing the three, you will have a sense of how each is used most effectively and when it might be appropriate to use one instead of another.

CHAPTER eight

Now I Have Evidence: Writing and Crafting Your Research

talking points

- How do I structure my essay's argument?
- Do I need to write an outline for my research paper?
- What should be included in that outline?
- When should I begin my bibliography?
- How should I structure my essay?

One big advantage of good note taking—something we have stressed several times throughout this book—is that you will be able to organize and outline your research paper much more efficiently with thorough notes in hand than if you have few or no carefully written notes at all. Instead of starting from scratch to figure out what in the world you will write, your note cards and various jottings should serve as the scaffolding on which you construct the first draft of your essay.

Crafting Your Argument

Elsewhere in this book, we have emphasized the importance of arguing accountably and effectively and defending your points of view. Now that it's time to begin writing, it is time to craft an effective argument—also known as the *thesis* of your paper, the overarching concern that you will defend.

An academic argument—again, as we've said before—is a kind of conversation with your readers. Although you may indeed have arguments with siblings, parents, and friends, we use the term "argument" in a positive, and not negative, way. There are three main components of an argument: the claim you are making, the reasons you are making the claim, and the evidence you are using to support that claim. That is, you will be making a claim and using examples appropriately to support it.

The Claim

Your claim is, obviously, the argument that is ultimately in the form of a thesis statement. If you have a research question, your claim will be the answer to that question. If you have a practical or conceptual problem that you are investigating, your claim may pose a solution to that problem.

For example: *The film* Jaws *helped to define a genre of film called the "natural disaster movie."*

Here's another example: *My father is a great caretaker.*

The Reasons

Your reasons support your claim through logic and by implying that you will have to defend this claim. Reasons give your audience cause to believe you. So, in following up this claim (written for a film as literature course), the writer might continue as follows: The film *Jaws* helped to define a genre of film called the "natural disaster movie" *because of its content, revealing the unpredictability of natural forces that one usually considers predictable.*

As you will see with this example, your reasons often use the word *because*: My father is a great caretaker *because he helps me get ready for school each morning.*

The Evidence

Your evidence serves as your proof. It supports your reasons, and your evidence will come from all of the data, research, fieldwork, or sources that you have gathered. In the case of this paper for a film class, consider the following:

> The film *Jaws* helped to define a genre of film called the "natural disaster movie" because of its content, revealing the unpredictability of natural forces that one usually considers predictable. *The film accomplishes this using traditional narrative devices such as surprise, suspense, and dramatic irony.*

> My father is a great caretaker because he helps me get ready for school each morning. *He makes me breakfast, he helps me get dressed, and he makes sure that I have all of my homework from the night before.*

Therefore, your claims, reasons, and evidence are all essential parts of your argument and your research essay. You will find that many arguments are structured as follows:

I believe (the claim) ➤ because of (the reason) ➤ based on (the evidence)

Make certain, therefore, that your argument follows this general structure.

Questions to Ask about Your Claim

- Is there an inappropriate bias? That is, you are taking a stand when you argue a point of view in your thesis. But are you revealing a bias that might be ill considered?
- Are you revealing a particular, possibly offensive agenda rather than a solid argument?
- Is your thesis statement (your argument, therefore) even arguable to begin with? That is, are you merely stating fact, or are you arguing a point of view?
- Is your claim too general? (You'll notice that some of these questions echo those in other chapters.)
- It there any audience to whom your argument will matter?
- When you read your thesis statement/argument, can you challenge yourself by saying "so what?" and have it spur you to defend it with logical evidence?

Questions to Ask about Your Reasons

- Are they logical? Do they "fit" with the argument you are trying to make?
- Do they reveal inappropriate bias rather than logical evidence?
- Do they adequately and soundly support your claim? How?
- How do your reasons connect with one another? Are they logically organized as part of your argument?
- Do you repeat your reasons without elaboration? If so, how can you revise these to make your reasons more effective?

Questions to Ask about Your Evidence

- Is your evidence credible? What types of sources have you used?
- Are there various perspectives and types of resources represented?
- Does your evidence truly support your arguments? How?

Being able to discern your claims from your reasons and your evidence is a first step toward organizing your research. For instance, you'll find that many research papers are outlined as follows:

Reason One
    Evidence to Support Reason One

Reason Two
    Evidence to Support Reason Two

Reason Three
    Evidence to Support Reason Three

. . . and so on.

The next section suggests ways to build your first draft, paying attention to the ways in which you not only create an effective argument but also organize it effectively.

Stop and Consider

We've just asked you to ask questions about your own argument. Now it's time to try your argument on a willing classmate at this pre-final stage (we'll ask you again later), especially if that classmate plays "devil's advocate." This means that your classmate will respond skeptically and try to find holes in your argument (saying "Who says?"), looking for reasons to doubt your evidence (when you discuss that after stating your argument) or anticipating the potential objections of your audience with counter-arguments you might have missed. Consider this a test-run for your writing, something akin to a focus group for your purpose. That said, analyze your classmate's feedback, testing it against your own knowledge of the subject and the argument, before you buy it!

Organizing and Strategizing

Therefore, before you begin writing, you should first organize all of the materials you will use to craft your outline—the road map for you as a writer, the results of which will guide your reader through your argument. Don't be afraid to take over the kitchen table or your dorm room floor. Although surrounding yourself with your many resources and notes may irritate your roommate, having a chance to survey everything visually—to take it all in, if you will—will help you begin working on a draft.

Part of the organization process also involves differentiating between ideas that you will glean from your many resources and ideas that you have been able to craft and to synthesize from your many hours poring over resources in the library, on the Internet, or wherever you have found (and made note of) them. Again, surveying all of the resources you have accumulated, and organizing them prior to drafting, will keep you credible and accountable—and on track. And consider that this type of review of your notes and resources may also help you determine whether there are any gaps that might send you back to the library or to the Internet.

From Notes to an Outline

Just as we urged you to do some pre-searching before you began crafting your research question, we also urge you to do some pre-writing before you begin the drafting process. Outlining, for instance, is a form of prewriting. As with any kind of essay writing, it is extremely helpful to do some kind of outlining to help you envision the paper, and this outline can take the form of a list, if you so choose.

The expectations for writing about a research question are no different than the expectations for any other essay—only higher. The audience will anticipate that you will clearly articulate your argument, support your argument through both your resources and your own ideas, and make use of those resources both ethically and credibly. So it is all the more important that you make sure to carefully and thoughtfully plan your research paper.

An outline will help you structure that work, and it will provide that all-important road map for you as you move forward with the writing process. That said, however, remember that some writers prefer to start drafting after they've organized their materials, turning to an outline or list (or précis, which we will discuss) when they find themselves stuck or in need of more planning. Writing is more often than not a nonlinear process.

Your outline may vary according to the nature of your particular assignment, but it should do the following:

> *Return to both your initial research question and thesis statement.*
> A good thesis statement, as we have discussed earlier in the book, should precisely and concretely articulate the argument that you intend to support in the essay. Including the thesis in your outline

will help you return to the framework you initially established for your research. Why were you originally interested in this topic? What did you want to explore? What questions did you want to answer? The answers to these questions—many of which you asked at the start of this project—should help guide you as you organize your paper.

Express both your argument and your supporting claims.
As you move into the writing stage of the research process, you will need to be able not only to give your argument but also to support your argument. Your outline should include all supporting claims and evidence in the order you wish for them to appear in the essay. In other words, make your argument, explain the reasons for your argument, and then provide your audience with evidence, which will mostly come from your resources. Typically, arguments tend to be ordered in sequence from weakest to strongest, so that your research paper ends in the strongest possible way before you tie together your work in the conclusion.

Include the ideas you want to integrate from each resource.
Your outline is the place where, if you have taken good notes throughout the research process, your hard work should begin to pay off. These notes will not only indicate which sources you will be citing from, but—if you followed our note card model in Chapter 3— these notes should also indicate exactly which of the concepts, ideas, and direct quotes from the source you will include in your paper.

Since the most useful outlines are usually concise, you won't need to include the full quotation or summary from the text. Instead, you will want to write something like "include quote from Smith, page 53," or "stuff from note card number 12," or "discuss Rich's theory of feminist poetics." The point is, of course, that your outline should indicate what you want to say and where you want to say it—and how.

Explain what you learned.

If you were conducting scientific research, you would want to make sure that the end of your outline makes note of the results of your study. However, since you're probably grappling with the kind of conceptual research topics we discussed in prior chapters, you likely won't be revealing or analyzing any quantitative data. Nonetheless, it is important that you begin to flesh out your concluding ideas. What did you find throughout the research process? What conclusions did you come to? What was revealed to you (and, in turn, to your audience)?

Keep in mind, moreover, that there is no one, single, desirable structure for an outline, unless your instructor requires a particular format. In what one of us calls "the old days," instructors would often demand a rigorous template: Begin with roman numeral "I," use subhead "A," followed by sub-subhead "1," and then lowercase "a," and so forth. You needn't—unless your instructor expects it, again—structure your outline in this way. Some writers use a topic-based outline; others use bullet points or sentences that remind them of the direction they wish to take.

The Anti-Outline

All that said, some of us find outlines not only difficult to do—acknowledging that writing is often a recursive process of discovery, that it is not linear—but counterproductive. In that case, consider writing a *précis* (pronounced prey-see) that encourages you to summarize what you believe your research paper will be about after you've reviewed and thought about all of your materials. Then, you can work backward, so to speak, from there: "If my summary says X and Y, then I will use A and B to begin to argue that point of view." You will need to be very familiar with your research materials and have some sense of the direction of your paper (something we recommend anyway) to do this.

Even if you are not writing a précis of your own essay, you can create a précis for most of the key entries in your bibliography, summarizing each of those articles or books or other sources concisely, clearly, and coherently. These summaries will help you think critically about how to best use these sources and incorporate them in your paper, and they will be useful if your instructor requests an annotated bibliography, a bibliography that features a short paragraph or so about each entry, delineating the main point(s) of the source and indicating its relevance to the overall topic and focus of the paper.

The bottom line: Sketch things out on paper (hand-written or digital) as a type of list or group of summaries that will help you draft your essay. Make sure it's a list that you can access with ease anytime you want to consult it—in a hard-copy notebook or on a jump drive or a tablet that you always have with you.

Begin with Your Bibliography—Standard or Annotated

The Standard Bibliography

Because students usually dread writing their bibliographies, they often save this task until the very end of the writing process, often throwing them together right before they submit the final essay to the instructor. (There is more information about bibliographies and citations in the next chapter.)

In truth, it is best to begin your bibliography during the initial stages of the research process. As we'll discuss in the chapter that follows, there are many online resources—which are both user friendly and free to the public—that you can use to track your sources as you collect them and that will also assist your putting these sources in the appropriate format. Since these online bibliographies are easy to amend, you can (and should) add and subtract from them as you refine your final lineup for your bibliography.

Starting the writing process with a working bibliography will not only help you keep mental track of the many texts from which you are summarizing, paraphrasing, and quoting, but having the bibliography will also help you write your in-text citations. In the next chapter, we discuss how you can format both your bibliography and your in-text citations (which we will discuss later).

So start your bibliography, print it out, and have it near you as you draft.

The Annotated Bibliography

As you write, you will want to ensure that you are able to articulate fully and carefully the ideas expressed in the resources you have chosen to include in your bibliography. In other words, before you begin incorporating a source in your essay draft, you want to first make sure that you can summarize its key points.

As we mentioned earlier, an annotated bibliography allows you to do just that. Annotated bibliographies include not only the requisite information necessary for a citation (author, publisher, dated published), but they also include a brief summary outlining main ideas.

Here's an example of an annotated citation:

Pollan, Michael. *The Omnivore's Dilemma: A Natural History of Four Meals*. Penguin Press, 2006.

> Pollan's book explores the paradox that is the American diet. He examines not only what we eat, but he also attempts to explain how we have devolved into a country that supports an unhealthy and unethical food system—one that isn't environmentally sustainable. Pollan approaches this book through an interdisciplinary lens, relying on history, science, and personal experience to make his argument.

Instructors will often ask for an annotated bibliography as part of the process toward your final research paper as a way to have you (and for the instructor) to examine the appropriateness and depth of your research. Sometimes this annotated bibliography is included with the final paper; this is up to your instructor.

Coming Up with a Title

Much like the bibliography, many students wait until the end of the writing process to come up with a title. Although you don't want to title your paper too soon—sometimes we don't know how things will turn out until we finish drafting—coming up with a working title at this point can help you focus your paper. Conversely, it can also help you test the evidence you'll use to defend your argument—and it may mean that you need to retool the title.

Furthermore, writers may find that a clear title will help get them started; having articulated a focus (even if it needs redoing later on) might help conquer the blank screen or page. Although there is no absolutely correct way to create a title, it has become customary in many disciplines to have a two-parter. That is, the first part preceding a colon is the attention-grabber, or the larger part of your argument, while the part after the colon is more specific. Here are some examples:

> Caffeine-Crazed: Race and Coffee Culture(s) in the United States
> Taming the Tyranny of Fashion: The Iconography of the High-Heeled Shoe

Of course, the colon is not mandatory, and to many, the two-part title has become something of a cliché. You can always craft a suitable title without the two-part format:

> Masculinity and the Cultures of Video Games in the 1980s
> The Decline of Female Professors in STEM Disciplines

Once you have a working title (remember, you can always change it, and it's likely that you will), you can begin the process of drafting your paper.

Planning and Drafting

Are you ready to begin writing? Perhaps. Perhaps the outline or précis (or sketch, or however you are conceptualizing your work) isn't even finished, but you find yourself just itching to start drafting the first part of your paper, and you want to see where your writing takes you. That's fine; for many, writing, as we've noted, is a very recursive and often non-linear process. But do as much of that outline as you can—just in case it helps you later on. And, indeed, if you're eager to give the writing a try, it could be just because you want to test the proverbial waters and see if you are, indeed, prepared to begin drafting the entire paper. (We will acknowledge that some of us actually begin to write "in our heads" once we have gathered and reviewed the research materials and generated the focus of the paper—and the main argument. This makes us ready to begin the drafting process, but of course, this isn't the case for everyone.)

RESEARCH

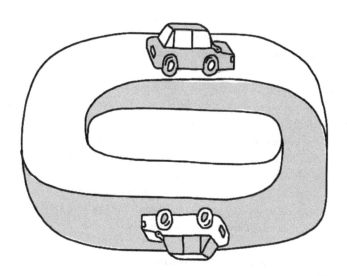

WRITING

You will know you might be ready to begin drafting your research essay when:

- You have spent a considerable amount of time gathering, surveying, and analyzing various resources.
- You have a developed and focused thesis statement or research question.
- You have considered what your thesis statement promises and whether you are able to "make good" on that promise.
- You have considered both your ethos as a research writer and the audience you are either explicitly or implicitly addressing through your work.
- You can identify not only your supporting arguments but also the evidence with which you will back your claims.
- You understand what you have learned as a researcher and what your audience will learn from reading your essay.
- You have written an outline (you may also call it a "list") that orders the various topics and sources that you will use to prove your argument.
- You understand and accept that you may not have the perfect introduction to your argument just yet: Sometimes you have to finish the paper to know what it is you'll be introducing, so don't let the introduction stop you. You can add that later.
- You find yourself eager to test all of the work you've done with a "dry run"; or, conversely, you aren't that eager. Either way, it might be time to see whether your materials are ready, your thesis is sound, and that your arguments and your evidence are well organized. It might just be time to plunge in.

Just as starting this project may have seemed overwhelming, so, too, will the blank page or screen seem overwhelming as you prepare to write. The hardest part, sometimes, is getting started. Be aware that even as you write, you will find yourself coming back, revising, changing, and moving the order of things. This is all part of most writers' processes. Save punctuation, style, and other, similar concerns for later; gather your materials and begin.

Initiating Conversation

Using your note cards, create a storyboard. That is, arrange these cards on a table—or, if you are using a tablet, arrange them on the desktop—as a way to see the best way for your notes to contribute to your overall plan. Laying these out visually may be helpful to you as you begin to work on your first draft. Think of these cards as a link in a chain of logic; move the links in this chain to make your evidence build most effectively. Share your storyboards with your classmates and ask for their input, articulating your overall strategy (that is, your argument) so that they can comment on the order of your evidence.

Creating the Body of Your Research

Although we understand that writing this type of project seems to be more daunting than other types of writing you may have done—especially because research essays are much longer than some other assignments and because they integrate ideas other than your own—ultimately, it's important to remember that even long research projects are structured in a similar fashion to other essays you may have written before.

That is, they will have an introduction (where you state your claim/ your argument/your thesis), a body (many paragraphs, not just several, where you provide your reasons and your evidence), and a conclusion (where you sum up your argument without introducing anything new).

Depending on what your instruction requires, you may wish to have subheadings for sections that depart topically from your other sections. You may also find that you will work on the body paragraphs of your paper before coming up with your introduction and conclusion. Why? Because as you write, you may find that your argument needs a bit of tweaking as you write about your evidence; consequently, your conclusion might be a bit different, too.

There are many ways to structure the body of your paper. Here are some possibilities, and some will work more effectively for certain topics and not others:

- Present your evidence in chronological order.
- Structure your evidence around a narrative (telling a story).
- Present your evidence in the order of least importance to most importance.
- Present your evidence in the order of least contentious to most contentious.
- Structure your evidence around what you assume your audience knows most to what it knows least.

Depending on the nature of your thesis, you may wish to structure your paper around one of the traditional modes (of which argument is one):

Comparison and Contrast
Cause and Effect
Definition

Ultimately, you will have to consider your topic and determine which is best for your particular research project. Most important, let the nature of your argument and your evidence supporting it guide your organizational choices.

Furthermore, whichever structure you choose, make sure to provide signposts for your reader throughout, using transitional words and phrases (first, last, next, consequently, however . . . and the like) that link your evidence and make the order of your reasons and supporting evidence clear. Once you have decided on the organizational structure of your paper and have created an outline (or anti-outline), you are ready to start integrating all of your evidence (your research).

As we have noted in Chapter 7, you will use direct quotation, paraphrasing, and summary to integrate your source material with your arguments. Remember, when drafting, to make sure that *your* analysis of the evidence is what guides the paper.

Ideas Into Practice

Now that you're aware of the annotated bibliography, take five or ten of your own sources and annotate them (remember your numbered note cards, whether paper or online) to illustrate to your instructor and to yourself what is important about them. Make sure to organize them in alphabetical order by the author's last name (just as you would in a standard bibliography).

Then, create an anti-outline, where you slate in order the annotated sources; this is also a good time to begin to figure out in what order these sources will appear in your work. Write several lines thinking through your decision-making process:

> For example, I'm going to begin with note card 3 that has the quote from Mark Twain about honesty. This will help draw in my reader as I begin to write about ethics.

Or:

> On page two, as I began my own discussion of trade agreements, I will paraphrase Bill Clinton's quote about the NAFTA trade agreement from note card 12. This will lead well into the political controversies surrounding his signing of the agreement.

In other words, you're doing the writing equivalent of "talking through" why you are making the choices you are making—a productive way to check yourself and your analysis of your resources. At the same time, you're actually developing a rough, outlined draft, if an incomplete one, that may prove useful to you later.

CHAPTER nine

What's Appropriate? Citing Sources and Citation Formats

talking points

- What are the various citation styles?

- Which style will I likely be using in my college writing class?

- What is a bibliography and how do I write one?

- In-text citations? What are those?

- What—exactly—needs to be cited?

- How do I cite a film? A book? An interview?

- Is it okay to use online citation guides?

In this chapter, we will provide you with a brief overview of academic documentation, focusing primarily on MLA and APA styles, respectively. The MLA style, recommended by the Modern Language Association, is most frequently used in disciplines within the humanities. It is the style that we personally have had the most experience with—both as teachers and as academics. It is also the style that you will likely be asked to use in many of your college writing courses.

However, many of you will have encountered the style format represented by the American Psychological Association (APA)—and possibly others as well.

Understanding Citations

It is important, therefore, to acknowledge that there are myriad citation styles that are commonly used in academic writing, depending on the discipline. And the goal of this particular chapter isn't necessarily to make you an expert in MLA, APA, or another style. Our goal, instead, is to help you understand *why* documentation is so important. To that end, we offer you an overview of some of these style formats rather than going into extensive detail about any one format in particular (see Table 9.1).

We also want to acknowledge that there are myriad resources online that will help you make certain that your bibliographic sources, your footnotes (if you have them), and your in-text citations are correctly formatted. As we hope and trust that you have reserved your intellectual energies for your thesis and your argument, we nonetheless want to help you be certain that you follow through on this important form of correctness and accountability. Citing your sources is important, and doing so correctly helps to establish your ethos.

Table 9.1   COMMON CITATION STYLES

STYLE	DISCIPLINES
MLA (Modern Language Association)	Literature, arts, humanities
APA (American Psychological Association)	Psychology, education, social sciences
AMA (American Medical Association)	Medicine, health, biological sciences
Turabian/University of Chicago	Various disciplines

That is, properly documenting your sources lets your readers know that you are accountable and credible. If you fail to cite your sources accurately, your readers may question your credibility, assuming that you are either being incautious, or, worse, dishonest.

Bibliographies, Works Cited, and References

There is one surefire way that you can easily identify a piece of research writing: there will always be a bibliography accompanying it. Because research writing always relies on something outside of the author's own ideas, you can look to the bibliography to see exactly what that something (or set of somethings) is. That is, the bibliography—or list of works cited or references, depending on the documentation style your instructor uses—lists the resources that a writer has used to craft his or her own research essay.

Although many will use these terms interchangeably, a bibliography is more often than not a comprehensive list of every source you consulted, whereas a works cited or references list refers only to those sources that you actually used in the paper. Some instructors will ask that you provide both kinds of lists—and some will also ask for an annotated bibliography that will not only explicate each source in brief but that will also indicate the value for each source related to your topic.

As is the case for in-text citations, which we will talk about a little later on in this chapter, the structure of your bibliographical citations will depend on which citation style you are using. Although there will be slight variations in the arrangement of information in each citation, depending on the style, most of the entries in your bibliography will have the same types of information—even if the citation style dictates that the information be presented in a different order. That is, nearly all bibliographical citations tell the reader the author (or editor) of the source, the title, and the date of publication.

In any documentation style, most citations begin with a name—either the name of a person (an author, editor, director, narrator, or similar) or the name of an organization (such as the American Association of Pediatrics). This lets the reader know who is responsible for having written or created the source. If the author is unlisted, the citation may begin with the source's title or an abbreviation of it.

MLA style follows an author-title format. That is, the second piece of information in MLA format will almost always be the title of the source. Let's look at an example of how we would create a bibliographical citation for a book with a single author, using MLA format:

Doe, Jane. *The Title of the Book*. Publisher, 2004.

You'll see that we have included four important pieces of information: the author, the title of the source, the publisher, and the date of publication.

APA style, in contrast, follows an author-date format. Because this style is mostly used in the sciences and social sciences, the date of publication is especially important. Researchers will need to know, in a way that is readily accessible, how long ago the data or study they are referencing was published, as information can change frequently in scientific fields. Let's look at how we might cite the same book, this time using APA style:

Doe, J. (2004). *The title of the book*. Location: Publisher.

Although the format has changed slightly, you will note that the bibliographic entry still contains the same basic information.

Stop and Consider

By this point, you should already have a lineup of credible and authoritative sources, which we trust you have evaluated carefully. Likely, many of those sources have their own bibliographies, some of which may vary in terms of usefulness for your purpose. Look at several of the bibliographies, comparing and contrasting similarities and differences among them, and letting your analysis inform the format and inclusion of different entries in your own work.

The figures that follow diagram the parts of a works cited entry (MLA style) and a references entry (APA style) for the same source.

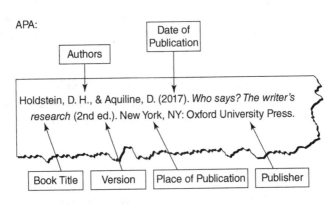

The sources you will cite in MLA or APA style may be journal articles by multiple authors, websites with no authors, video games, paintings, or government reports. Our aim in this book isn't to provide you with examples of how to cite every kind of source. Instead, along with very basic information about these two major citation styles, our aim is to help you understand *why* bibliographic citations are so important—and what basic information should be included across styles.

As you have read elsewhere in this book, the bibliography isn't something that you really save until the very end of the project. You will have been looking at sources from the very beginning, and consequently, you will have been building your works cited list—although it appears at the end of the paper—from the very start.

When Should You Begin Creating Your Bibliography?

However you choose to organize your notes and information regarding your sources—your iPad, the notes feature on your smartphone, hand-written note cards, or the like—we have emphasized that it's essential to record and to record accurately the sources of your materials as soon as you find them. As we've indicated before, you can conceivably begin your actual bibliography, your official list of sources, as soon as you begin your research, saving both time and stress at the end.

Earlier, we mentioned online resources that aid in creating bibliographies. Sites such as *EasyBib*, *BibMe*, and *KnightCite* (and although such sites seem to come and go with frequency) help to create and save bibliographical citations. Using these various resources allows to you easily amend your bibliographical list whenever necessary. So, if you add a source to your bibliography and later decide that you won't be using it for your essay, you can always delete it. Remember that it's always easier to delete a source than it is to scramble to find the citation for a source you decide in the last minute that you need to include. (In fact, we even recommend keeping a "deleted source list" on your notepad or hard drive, just in case, or maintaining all of your sources on your note cards or their equivalent, even after you've assembled a working bibliography.)

The In-Text Citation

Having a working bibliography to use as a reference as you write your essay will also help you when it comes to in-text citations (the format for which we will be talking about next). In-text citations are notes, located within the body of your research essay, that let your readers know what sources you are quoting, summarizing, or paraphrasing within your own paper. These are also important to your credibility, as they hold you accountable for crediting the original sources.

In both MLA and APA styles, part or all of your in-text citations will almost always be formatted within parentheses. Your bibliography not only organizes your sources in alphabetical order, but the individual bibliographic entries are also good indicators of what piece of information needs to come inside your parenthetical citations. Almost always, the piece of information that appears first in your bibliography—whether it is a title, a director's name, the editorial name, or the name of an author—is what belongs in your in-text citations.

For example, let's say the following is a source listed in your bibliography:

Gold, Janet. *Why Bibliographies Are Useful.* Good Research Press, 2003.

In this case, the very first piece of information is the author's last name. Therefore, a parenthetical citation in MLA format would look something like this: (Gold 23).

Say, instead, your bibliographical listing looked like this:

"Being an Accountable Researcher." *English Student Magazine,* May 2012, pp. 23–28.

In this particular entry, you can see that there is no identifiable author of the article. So, rather than the author's last name, the in-text citation—again, in MLA format—would include the title of the article: ("Being an Accountable Researcher" 25).

Quick Fact

What we now call the *MLA Handbook* (Eighth Edition, no less, at 146 pages) was first conceived as the *MLA Style Sheet*, primarily as a way to prepare manuscripts for publications. The modern-era *MLA Handbook* evolved from its then-new incarnation in 1971, and was most recently revised in 2016 to emphasize common features across all source types. MLA's 2016 update attempts to simplify the documentation process for writers and to make it easier for readers to find a writer's sources.

MLA:

The authors argue that this information is true (Holdstein and Aquiline 123).

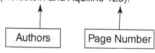

APA:

The authors argue that this information is true (Holdstein & Aquiline, 2016, p. 123).

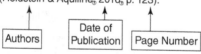

Initiating Conversation

Compare the draft of your research paper, even if it is not yet complete, with one of the papers included in the book. Make note of the sample paper's use of citation, whether it is MLA, APA, or another format. Which format are you planning to use for your citations? How will you have to configure your in-text citations, based on the examples you read in the book?

Formatting In-Text Citations

In-text citations are just as they sound: citations that are placed within the body of your essay. They are visual and logical markers, indicating to your reader when and where you are integrating intellectual material from one of your sources, whether directly quoted or not. In short, they signify when you are using ideas or words that are not your own.

Therefore, in a research paper, it is common to have many in-text citations, although one is warned (again) not merely to string quotations and citations together and avoiding the kind of "patchwriting" we discussed earlier in this book. In fact, while we always tell our students that it is best to err on the side of excess—in other words, if in doubt, use a citation—we reiterate that there is also a need to balance the number of quotations or citations in the essay with your own, appropriately conceived words. Most instructors will forgive an extra citation or two. However, if you forget to use a citation where one is needed, that mishap could be mistaken for plagiarism.

Although we stated earlier that in-text citations in MLA and APA styles are enclosed within parentheses, in-text citations can also be presented as footnotes.

And when you hear the word "footnote," keep in mind that one type of footnote is used in some formats, albeit rarely, instead of (and in place of) in-text, parenthetical citations; however, in most forms of scholarly writing, the footnote is used as a way to provide additional explanation or to amplify a point made within the body of the essay or article. In this book, we write only of internal, parenthetical citation forms, as we expect that these will be the ones you will be required to use.

To reiterate: in the MLA format, your parenthetical citation will usually include the author's last name and the page number on which you found the ideas you discuss in any particular part of your essay. APA format, however, includes the author's last name and the publication date of the source you have referenced. (Remember, publication dates are particularly important within scientific disciplines.)

Let's look more specifically at some of the various occasions for citing sources, using both MLA and APA formats.

A Single Author

As noted in our earlier examples, most of the time, you will be working with resources that have a single author. Single-author citations are, moreover, the simplest to document. Depending on the style format, you will include either the last name and the page number, or the last name, the publication date, and a page number of the particular source:

> *MLA Example:* (Johnson 213)
> *APA Example:* (Johnson, 1992, p. 213)

Note: Although APA format doesn't require a page number for all citations—only when directly quoting a source—we find it to be a good idea to include one anyway. Fortunately, APA allows this as an option, one we prefer.

Two Authors

If a source has two authors, you will include both names each time you reference the source in your text, listing them alphabetically.

> *MLA Example:* (Adams and Goldblatt 297)
> *APA Example:* (Adams & Goldblatt, 2007, p. 297)

Three or More Authors: MLA Style

In MLA style, if a source has three or more authors, you will only include only the first author's name followed by "et al." ("and others" in Latin) any time you reference the source in your text.

Example: (Fowler et al. 34–40)

Three to Five Authors: APA Style

In APA style, if a source has three to five authors, you will cite all of these authors the first time you reference the source in your text. In additional references to that source, include only the first author's name followed by "et al."

> *First Use Example:* (Teran, Jenkins, Ng, & Smith, 2016, pp. 5–7)
> *Subsequent Use Example:* (Teran et al., 2016, pp. 5–7)

Six or More Authors: APA Style

In APA style, if a source has six or more authors, you will only include only the first author's name followed by "et al." ("and others" in Latin) any time you reference the source in your text.

> *Example:* (Patel et al., 2014, p. 197)

Unknown Author

If an author's name is not listed—and this means that one is not provided at all, not that you can't find it—then you would include the title of the source inside of the parenthetical citation. If the title is long, it is acceptable to just use the first few words of the title. Remember, you must format the title appropriately, using either italics or quotation marks.

> *MLA Example:* ("Global Warming and Factory Farming" 26)
> *APA Example:* ("Global Warming and Factory Farming," 2001, p. 26)

Some Additional Tips about Formatting In-Text Citations

- If there is no page number on this original source, which often happens with online sources and websites, then you are not expected to include a page number in the citation.

- It is acceptable to include a span of pages in the citation. For example, if you were discussing ideas from pages 120–123 of a book by Emily Wong, your parenthetical citation would look like this in MLA style: (Wong 120–23) or like this in APA style: (Wong, 2002, pp. 120–123). If you are using a direct quote, however, you should include the specific page citing the location of that quote. And you generally wouldn't want to span more than five pages in one citation. Remember, you always want to make it easy for your readers to trace the information you've cited back to the original source.

- Parenthetical citations are always a part of the sentence and never a part of the quotation. In other words, the punctuation for your sentence should come *after* the citation. Example: There is a direct correlation between the number of fast food restaurants in a community and the obesity rate (Porter 32).

- However, if you are directly quoting a source, the quotation marks should close *before* the citation begins. Example: White argues that "making sure people have access to healthy food choices is a community's responsibility" (129).

- If you use a signal phrase to introduce a quotation, that is, stating the author's name in a sentence (as we did in the example earlier), then you are not required to restate the name in the parenthetical citation. Instead, just put the page number (for MLA) or the publication date and page number (for APA).

- If a direct quotation is longer than four lines of prose in MLA style, or is 40 words or more in APA style, then the quote should be formatted into what is called a "block quote." That is, indent the quotation as in the following example, in which the writer quotes from the Norton Critical Edition of Emily Brontë's *Wuthering Heights*.

> Brontë chooses to reveal this information in summary, not in action: Heathcliff went up once, to show her Linton's will. He

had bequeathed the whole of his, and what had been her, moveable property to his father. The poor creature was threatened, or coaxed, into that act during her week's absence, when his uncle died. (223)

- MLA and APA style both ask for double spacing throughout a text, including block texts. They should be evenly spaced before, within, and after the text that surrounds them. Both MLA and APA also require the same degree of indentation—one inch or approximately five character spaces. This is the same degree of indentation that a new paragraph uses in the paper.
- You need not add quotation marks around block quotes; the fact of the block itself signifies its being a quotation. Remember: The name of the author would usually precede the page number—223—but the author's name (Brontë) was mentioned in the signal phrase that introduced the quote. You can also omit the author's name from repeated citations of the same source when no other sources have been quoted in the interim.

In-Text Citations and the Academic Conversation

In-text citations serve a larger role within academic communities in addition to the function they serve in your paper. Not only do they hold you accountable as the research writer, but they also allow readers of your work to follow up on any particular resources that may interest them.

For instance, let's say that Professor X writes a research essay about climate change and the resulting effects on coastal communities in Alaska. Professor Y might read the essay, find a specific section that particularly interests her, and decide that she wants to know more. By looking at the in-text citation that Professor X originally included in his work, Professor Y is now able to identify the book, article, or multimedia resource from which this highly interesting idea originated.

This is a scholarly cycle we have mentioned many times throughout this book, and, by conducting and writing research, you are playing a key role in that cycle. Using citations appropriately and carefully will assure that your readers—and other scholars—are able to use your research as a springboard for their own.

What Needs to Be Cited?

You must cite *anything* and *everything* that has come from a resource. Any form of intellectual property must be honored by an in-text citation. So, regardless of whether you are directly quoting, paraphrasing, or summarizing, if the information did not come from you, you must cite it.

You will include a citation when you use:

- the original language from a source
- ideas from a source that you have put in your own words via paraphrasing or summary
- individual facts
- specific phrasing
- unique terminology
- any visual materials from a source (photographs, cartoons, charts, graphs, etc.)
- ideas from a speech, lecture, or interview
- ideas from a television show, movie, or documentary

Online Citation Guides

One of the reasons that we have chosen to provide such a brief overview of citation styles is that we acknowledge that so many citation resources are now readily available online. Citation guides—regardless of the style—are constantly updated and amended. So, in many ways, online resources—which can be updated easily and frequently—will often provide the most relevant and timely information when it comes to the various documentation formats.

Your instructor will likely point you in the direction of some reliable and credible online guides. (Remember our conversation about online resources from earlier in the book?) However, simply conducting a Google search for "MLA format" or "APA style" will yield multiple results, many of which will be of use to you.

Even more specifically, when you have questions about citation styles for a particular kind of source, Google may also come in handy. Searching for "how to cite a documentary in MLA format" or "how to cite an interview in Turabian" will often lead to the answers you are looking for.

In addition, many of the websites for your schools' libraries will include helpful information about citation styles.

So, as we have already mentioned, and as you likely know, the Internet can be an invaluable tool when it comes to academic documentation.

Ideas Into Practice

In the following list, we've deliberately left off any quotation marks, italics, citations, or indications of citation formatting—and in some instances, we've left out the year the document or other item was published or produced. Use whatever citation format your instructor prefers and/or an appropriate online resource, and put the following in correct bibliographic format, researching any missing information as needed.

If you like, think of this as a bibliographic scavenger hunt of sorts:
Any essay in Best American Essays, 1986
Abbey Road, the Beatles, 1969, Apple Corps

Alfred Hitchcock's Psycho
I Have a Dream (speech, not text)
Address Given on Inauguration Day, 1961
Season four, episode 12 of I Love Lucy
Interview with Barack and Michelle Obama by Barbara Walters
The Feminist Fertility Myth, Slate, December 2012
Car Talk's final radio episode
Halo, Version 1, Xbox
Cover story, Ladies' Home Journal, March 1932

CHAPTER ten

What Now?
Revising, Presenting, Reviewing

talking points

- I'm done writing—now what?

- How can I revise my essay?

- What is peer review?

- What should I take into consideration when turning my essay in to my instructor?

- My instructor wants me to create a presentation based on my research. What questions should I consider?

- What visual tools will help me best communicate my work? What pitfalls should I avoid?

Throughout this book, we have frequently discussed the various processes involved in writing about research: there is a process for choosing a topic, a process for gathering research, and a process for writing the research paper. As you approach the finish line, try not to lose sight of these processes, which, admittedly, don't necessarily follow in a straight line. That is, you might find yourself generating new content just as you've finished revising another section of your paper; you might find that you need to revise your introduction after you've made it to the conclusion; and so on.

And just because you have finished typing the conclusion, your research essay isn't necessarily complete.

The truth is, as much as we have encouraged you to engage with your instructors and your fellow researchers as you work through your projects, research writing can be—and often is—a solitary act. Ultimately, though, you have to make sure that your work is appropriate for a larger audience—whatever audience that may be.

So the final steps—the ones you will work through even after you may think you are "done"—are as important as any other. Before your research is prepared to make its debut, you must revise, review, and thoughtfully consider (and reconsider) the best methods for your written work along with the possibility of a presentation format of the same (or most of the same) information.

Revising

You might also want to approach your writing process, and consequently, your revising process, by thinking about both higher order concerns (HOCs) and lower order concerns (LOCs). HOCs are the more important and often more global areas of concern, such as idea development, clarity, focus, and purpose. LOCs, on the other hand, are instances that will likely be corrected during the editing of your essay (correcting word choices and commas, for instance), which will, in most cases, happen last. When editing for LOCs, you'll be looking to assure that you have a technically sound essay, free of mechanical and grammatical errors, and with appropriate word choices and structurally sound paragraphs.

Higher Order Concerns

You likely will want to begin by addressing HOCs. In a research essay, in particular, your HOCs will determine whether you have been successful in communicating and supporting your argument, organizing and developing your ideas, and integrating your source material into your essay.

Remember, writing a research paper is much like having a conversation, albeit a fairly formal one, both with scholars and with your audience. Now that your essay is drafted, you will want to begin asking yourself whether you are effectively participating in those conversations.

As you test your research and your writing, you may find that switching roles—imagining yourself as the audience for your essay and not the author of your essay—can be an effective way of determining whether you have written an essay that will meet the various needs of your readers.

Consider those HOCs, asking yourself the following questions:

- Have I clearly articulated my argument in thesis form? (Have I tried to distance myself from the thesis and asked, "So what?" Is my answer to that question satisfactory?)
- Am I able to adequately support my argument, using both my own ideas and ideas from my resources?
- Is my essay focused? Do I stay on task for the entire length of the paper, avoiding any digressions or tangents?
- Do I use transitions between ideas and between paragraphs?
- Are my paragraphs logical and structured well?
- Have I developed my paragraphs logically?
- Does each paragraph harken back to my overall thesis?
- Have I integrated my sources appropriately, avoiding quotes that are merely strung together?

- Is there enough "me" in the argument—that is, enough of my own commentary on the subject, balanced with appropriate attribution and quotation of sources?
- Have I avoided an abrupt ending to the paper, instead crafting a conclusion that summarizes my overall argument?
- Is my choice of language appropriate for my audience? How so?
- Have I made certain to avoid introducing new ideas or arguments at the point of the conclusion?

Lower Order Concerns

Once you are confident that your research essay satisfies all of the HOCs, you will want to focus on LOCs. This sort of editing will likely be the final step in the writing process, completed a day or two before the final essay is due. Although we're all familiar with the occasional need to wait until the last minute before assignments are due, it's undoubtedly best, especially when working on a comprehensive research paper, to leave yourself plenty of time— and especially at the end of the process. This way, you can wait a few days after you've completed the paper, giving yourself a bit of "distance," so that you're more likely to catch surface errors and other LOCs.

Additional Strategies

As with any kind of writing, you will want to read through your essay several times, employing whatever proofreading strategies have worked for you in the past. Here are several editing strategies—strategies specifically designed to address LOCs— that we have used both with our students and with our own writing. Although this list isn't meant to be exhaustive, we hope it will help you get started:

Read Your Essay Aloud

It seems to be the case that whenever we ask students to read their work aloud in class, they stumble over several of their own errors. When we read our own work out loud, we often are able to identify many of the typos, grammatical mistakes, and punctuation errors that we would otherwise overlook when quickly scanning our essay and "reading it" in our heads.

So, as silly as it may seem, read your essay out loud either to yourself or to a roommate. Doing so will often help you "hear" and find places where you will need to make adjustments or corrections—and your listener may be able to help.

Read Your Essay with a Particular Edit in Mind

Because LOCs are so wide ranging, it can be very difficult to try to catch and to edit all of the missteps in your essay with a single reading. After all, how can you expect to identify spelling errors, misplaced commas, and incorrect citations all at the same time? It's likely that you can't. (For that matter, neither can we.)

So, instead, read through your essay with a very specific editing goal. For example, if you know that you have a tendency to misuse commas, read through your essay and *only* pay attention to comma usage. Or, if you want to be certain that you have correctly cited all of your resources using MLA format, read through your essay and *only* look at your citations. Although you may catch other errors and make them for a return visit, you won't initially be trying to do everything at once.

The point is this: the more you refine what specific changes or corrections you may need to make, the more likely you are to find those specific instances. Don't overwhelm yourself by trying to do it all at once.

Exchange Essays with a Classmate for Peer Review

No one knows the assignment for which you are writing better than your classmates. Like you, they have also spent the past several weeks sitting through class lectures, talking with your instructor, and working on their own research projects.

Therefore, when it comes time for you to revise and edit your complete draft, why not consult one of your peers? It is always a good idea to have another set of eyes read through your work before you turn it in, and you can return the favor by reading through your classmate's essay, too.

GUIDELINES FOR PEER REVIEW

1. Does the introduction center mostly around the writer's own analysis or does the writer rely too heavily on resources at the start of the paper? How can this be improved? How can the writer's ethos be established from the beginning?
2. Identify the argument/thesis within the introduction. How effective is it? Is it something can the writer should be able to prove?
3. Has the writer provided substantial background information to situate the argument? How so? How not?
4. In the body of the paper: Are you able to readily discern both the reasons and the evidence for this argument? Are there any places where more evidence is needed?
5. Is there fluid integration of source material? How? Are there good transitions between the writer's analysis and the source material? Are there any areas where there seem to be strings of quotes rather than analysis with integrated quotes? Where? What should be done to improve this?
6. Is every direct quote supported by a "quote sandwich?" Identify areas that need improvement, if any.
7. Are there effective transitions between ideas and paragraphs? If there are subheadings or sections in the body of the paper, are the transitions to these effective? How so or how not?

8. Are in-text citations formatted appropriately, according to whatever citation style the assignment requires? Point out strengths and weaknesses in this regard.

9. Are there any places that seem to be missing a citation? Make note of any information that needs to be credited to a source but is not. (Better to be safe than sorry; if you're not sure, ask.)

10. Are ample and appropriate forms of evidence sustained throughout the paper? Identify areas where the writer is particularly strong in providing convincing evidence that suits the argument; conversely, point out areas that need strengthening.

11. Does the paper conclude effectively? That is, does the writer sum up his or her arguments without redundancy and without introducing new information? Does the conclusion adequately reflect the thesis/argument of the entire paper? How so, or how not?

12. Check the writer's bibliography. Make sure the citations are formatted correctly, and make sure that everything cited in the paper is included there.

When revising either your essay or a classmate's essay during peer review, try to assess the work in stages, first paying attention to those HOCs and then, once you are confident that the essay is nearly complete, editing for LOCs.

So, as you approach your draft and work—or someone else's—to revise it, whether in class, online, or through other methods, consider these questions to test it: Have you presented your argument clearly and thoroughly? Is your choice of language suited to the argument and audience? Are your paragraphs well organized, stemming logically from your thesis statement? Are your sentences grammatically correct, and have you edited for surface features (spelling and the like)?

Stop and Consider

Earlier, you read about the rhetorical situation. The genres of academic writing demand particular conventions and language. Look over your draft, and in addition to the guidelines for peer review, consider the tone, diction, style, and overall rhetorical appropriateness of your writing. Are you attuned to your potential (and often complex) audience? Have you abstained from framing your research in too personal a perspective? Are you aware of your audience? How does your language, organization, and the like reflect this? Look at your own draft alongside some of your sources. While the style and tone might be different, some well-written pieces might well inspire you as you revise.

Taking One Last Look at Your Thesis

Throughout the research process, and even as you write the first draft of your research essay, you will find yourself refining and revising your ideas. This is a necessary part of research writing, and this sort of revision is a habit of all good writers.

So, as you begin to finalize your essay, you will want to look back at your starting point: your thesis statement. Your thesis statement was initially crafted at the onset of your research. And, though you may have tinkered with it as you delved further into your various resources, you might still need to look at your thesis in light of your final essay.

When reviewing your thesis statement, consider the following:

- Does your thesis express a clear and declarative argument? How so?
- Do the resources you include in your essay provide evidence in support of your argument? How so?
- Have you narrowed and focused the thesis as much as possible? (Often the scope of your argument will narrow further and further throughout the research process.) Really?

- If someone else were to read your thesis statement and say, "So what?" and can still find an argument that's worth reading about, then you just might be on to something. If the "so what?" leads to indifference (unless you've happened upon someone who is just apathetic about everything), then you might want to take another, careful look.

Answering "yes" to these questions and being able to defend that "yes" likely indicates that you have a thesis that suits your final essay.

Presenting Your Research

As we mentioned earlier in this chapter, there comes a time in every research process when the work must be introduced to an audience. Sometimes that audience may only be your instructor. However, other times, you will be asked to present your research to a larger audience of your peers.

Research presentations can take many forms, and deciding what kind of presentation best suits both your project and your audience is, perhaps, the most important step. Therefore, when preparing a research presentation, ask yourself two questions: How can I best communicate the ideas in my work to a specific and targeted audience? And what presentation tools—multimedia or otherwise—are best suited to my topic, my audience, and the occasion for which I am presenting? As you approach these questions, it will be helpful to reflect back on our conversation about rhetorical situations earlier in this book, along with our conversations about the benefits and pitfalls of the many multi- and social media options available to you.

Just as you must be savvy navigators of search engines such as Google and wary of advertisements and other information online, you must be equally savvy in the way you approach such presentation tools as Google Slides, PowerPoint, Prezi, and the like. No visual tool is better than a weak or distracting use of these tools.

There is nothing more inappropriate or boring than the rote use, for instance, of software such as PowerPoint when it adds little to nothing of value to a presentation. That is, let's remember that the purpose of multimodal tools is to give your audience a way to enhance your words—not to compete with your words or to undermine them. Therefore, copying and pasting full paragraphs of your research paper on to a poorly-designed PowerPoint presentation and reading it word for word does not offer such enhancement. And this is but one example of inappropriate use of this technology.

Just as you must work to establish your ethos in your written work, you must also maintain that credibility through the quality and appropriateness of your choices should you decide to use visual tools.

As we begin asking questions about what type of presentation might be appropriate for your topic, keep in mind the standard advice you might receive in a public speaking course. That is as follows:

- put as much time and effort into your presentation as you would an essay;
- consider what tools might best communicate to your audience, or if no visual tool is preferable;
- practice, rehearse your speech and your coordination with any visual materials;
- be clear and concise;
- remember that the spoken version of your paper could be quite different from your research paper; for instance, make sure your audience can follow your argument and highlight aspects of your work, not all of it;
- avoid any silly and unrelated visuals (no need to include that amusing picture of a cat) that potentially cheapen your points.

Ultimately, your goal is to highlight the most important aspects of your work and, in effect, summarize its argument and most cogent points, not to provide the equivalent of a laundry list of your entire paper.

Therefore, as you begin to devise a game plan for your research presentation, here are some questions to consider.

What Is the Nature of the Presentation?
Are you presenting as part of a small conference, fair, or program that requires you to set up a visual display of your research? Or are you being asked to give a five- to ten-minute summary presentation to your classmates? Clearly, your strategies will be different for each situation.

What Tools Are Best Suited to the Occasion for Which You Are Presenting?
If you are asked to set up a display at a small conference or research fair, you will likely make use of visual materials such as sophisticated poster boards, pamphlets, and brochures. However, if you are

asked to do a timed presentation at the front of your class, you might want to consider using multimedia tools—like PowerPoint, Prezi, or iMovie—to help you communicate the most essential information from your research.

Which Multimedia Tools Are Most Appropriate for the Location in Which You Are Presenting?

You don't want to spend hours creating a striking video about your research topic if the classroom in which you will showcase your work does not have the technology to support your using that video as part of your presentation. When considering which multimedia tools you would like to use, make sure you speak with your instructor about the classroom's limitations and opportunities as a presentation space.

What Multimedia Tools Are You Comfortable Using?

This may seem counterintuitive, but your research presentation may not be the best opportunity to take creative risks.

That is, although it is important that you push yourself to make use of multimedia tools that can enhance your presentation and interest your audience, it is also important that you choose a tool that you can use effectively and efficiently. You don't want to find yourself getting so frustrated by a new presentation format that you lose sight of the quality of information you are presenting. This is all to say: keep your eye on the ball. The most important aspect of your presentation should be your research, not your video-making skills. So work to find a balance between using a new and innovative form of media and presenting your research accurately and thoroughly. Remember, the power may go out, but the fire of your research should not.

What Does Your Audience Already Know about Your Topic?

Most research presentations give a significantly abbreviated overview of the work. Therefore, you will want to present the major points of your research, focusing on the aspects of your topic that the audience

151

won't already know. Ask yourself this: What does my audience already know about my topic? Are you speaking to a group of experts in the field related to your work? Or are you speaking to a more general audience? Is it necessary that you provide some background information? Although you should provide the context necessary to foster your audience's understanding of your work, you should also be as concise as possible.

Keep your specific audience in mind when deciding what information you should or shouldn't include in your presentation.

How Can the Presentation Complement the Research?

Your presentation is an opportunity to bring in visual materials (images, video clips, excerpts from interviews, music, and the like) that are not readily conveyed in hard copy. Take advantage of the presentation to offer something that is not readily developed in the essay, moving beyond presenting excerpts of the text itself.

Therefore, while we have encouraged you to present the most salient points of the essay, take the opportunity to go a bit beyond for the purposes of a live presentation. For instance, digital versions of magazines such as *The New Yorker* make available related content such as interviews, videos, and photographs online that are not available with the print version of a story and that extend the story itself.

To reiterate: Consider both your topic and your audience as you select the most appropriate way to convey salient information about your work in a presentation format. No matter the format or software—a poster board, Prezi, or movie-making software—the underlying principles of a good and sound presentation are the same. Know your audience, be prepared to convey the most important aspects of your research, and, if you use various media formats, be certain that they will be supported in your classroom and that they enhance but do not compete with the importance of your work.

....

Initiating Conversation

Using your classmates as a focus group, ask what visual materials—graphs, videos, photographs, and the like—would enhance or contribute to their understanding of your informational presentation. (Depending on your topic, be sure to discuss whether visual materials are necessary at all.) Sort through their suggestions on your own and incorporate the ones that you find to be most useful. You might also want to write a short essay or open letter to your class in which you respond to their suggestions and explain how you chose to use certain ideas (and which ones you did not use, and why).

....

Communicating Your Data or Research Visually

If you have the opportunity to present your research, the form of this presentation will to a good extent depend on your content. A presentation of a literature paper, for instance, might include PowerPoint slides showing photographs of authors and brief biographies; on the other hand, a science paper on regional weather data might include PowerPoint slides, but showing pie graphs, charts, and maps of the United States along with images of weather patterns.

Although you've likely used PowerPoint for various presentations in the past and are comfortable integrating visual images, audio clips, and the like into your presentations, research essays may also necessitate your using tables, graphs, and charts to best communicate evidence that is data driven.

When you use these tools, try to follow one simple rule: Never let your technology or graphic be more complex than your evidence or data. *In other words, keep it as simple as your research allows.* For instance, if you are presenting data about population shifts of zombies in Chicago, Illinois, in the 1970s, a simple table may suffice. (The point here is the graph, not our choice of subject.)

In contrast, if you want to emphasize differences and contrasts—fluctuating differences in pay between men and women over the past fifty years, for instance—then a bar graph might be the best choice, as it will visually illustrate the discrepancies as a complement to your discussion in writing.

Moreover, a pie chart might best illustrate the distribution of funds by percentages in the budget of a not-for-profit organization. These are but a few examples of visual ways of representing information, and the point, of course, is not to introduce you to the myriad ways you can visually communicate your data through tables, graphs, and charts. Rather, we urge you to take the time to survey your options and choose the graphics that best suit your information, your presentation, and your audience.

Tips for Creating Effective Visual Presentations:

Just because everyone seems to use PowerPoint doesn't mean that you have to do so. You can show a relevant graph and a chart if those illustrate most effectively, and simply, a point you want to make.

Nonetheless, many students tend towards slide shows as the most familiar (but not necessarily most effective) means of adding visuals to a presentation. Therefore, here are some guidelines to consider when crafting a slide-style (PowerPoint, Prezi, etc.) presentation:

1) **Keep it simple.** Whether we are talking about color scheme, aesthetics, the amount of information you want to include on a slide, or the number of slides, don't overwhelm your audience or your presentation. Remember that the purpose of visuals is to enhance your presentation, not to compete with it.

2) **Become friends with bullets (not that kind).** While you must write cohesive, detailed paragraphs in your research paper, your job here is to pull out the most important information to highlight it

for your audience who won't expect or want to read your paper on screen. Your main point can be on screen in the form of a bullet, and the rest of the related information should come from you.

3) **Don't read your slides!** Use the slides as guidelines, as prompts, or as starting points for your remarks so that your audience will remember your main point as you provide the rest of the information through your presentation.

4) **Judiciously mix visual text with alphabetic text.** Although simple, your slides should be elegant—but visually interesting. Aim to include some text and a bit of graphic on most slides. Eschew the cluttered. Make sure each slide is readable.

5) **Select only visuals that are relevant to and worthy of your topic.** As we noted earlier, all too many presentations are undermined by irrelevant, sometimes cutesy visual inserts that distract the audience and detract from the importance of your work.

6) **Speak slowly, and give your audience time to take notes and ask questions.** Although this information is not new to you, it might be new to your audience. Further, if you'd like members of the audience to save questions for the end, ask them to do so before you begin and suggest that they jot down their thoughts for the question-and-answer time at the end of your presentation.

7) **Connect the dots for your audience.** That is, explain how you came to your argument and your conclusions. Share some of your sources; why they interested you; surprising things you might have discovered on your way to looking for other things. This is a particularly good way to connect your visual material to your presentation—and is valuable even if you choose not to use visual material.

8) **Be credible.** Just as you have to be credible and accountable in your paper, so, too, must you be credible in your presentation. Where do your visuals, if you use them, come from? Make sure to cite the information in your presentation just as you would in your essay, with a list at the end or with a footnote on each slide.

9) **Be wary of infographics.** Although such graphics are ubiquitous on social media feeds and on the Internet, be sure they are reliable before you use them. Be certain that your graphics are derived from your research—and not the other way around.

For instance, if your research concerns equal pay for women soccer players, don't just Google "equal pay infographic," hoping that you will find an image that makes your argument for you. Instead, work to find an infographic that suits your research focus, or, better yet, create your own using statistics that you have found in reliable sources. After all, if you've done your due diligence, you will know enough about your topic to discern good from less good.

The Final Checkup

Before you submit the final draft of your essay to your instructor, you will want to review your full project one last time, making sure that you have all the necessary components of the assignment and that you have presented the various components professionally. Ensuring that your project is presented appropriately—that all of your t's are crossed and your i's are dotted, if you will—contributes to your ethos as a responsible student and a trustworthy researcher. (Your instructor may begin to question your ethos, however, if you turn in your final paper with a coffee mug stain on the first page.)

As you do this final review, consider the following questions as you also review our advice throughout this book:

- Do you need a cover page? If so, what information should be included on the cover page?
- Is there a title that is both attention getting and informative?
- Are all parenthetical citations formatted appropriately?
- Are there any missing citations—information that should be accounted for but is not?

- Are your pages numbered?
- Have you included your bibliography? And is that bibliography formatted correctly?

Conclusion

Your instructor will undoubtedly have certain ways of assigning and supporting ways of conducting research appropriately and usefully, ways that pique your intellectual curiosity as a budding researcher. In any event, the principles of careful, accountable research will carry beyond the classrooms through which you find yourself practicing its tenets, making you a more accountable, discerning citizen in the process.

Ideas Into Practice

Let's say you need to communicate aspects of your research paper to different types of audiences and through various media. In all these cases you must be fully aware of the unique rhetorical situation demanded by each.

> *How might you communicate the central ideas of your research paper as the following?*

As a pamphlet for young adults?

As a conversation with a family member—with no background in the topic—across the kitchen table?

As a multimedia presentation—a Web page, a Prezi, or a Power-Point—for your classmates?

As an instructional video of your research, including voice-overs, visual evidence, and presentation of quantitative data, for instance, for an educated, general audience?

As a summary memorandum to an executive who is interested in your ideas?

157

Appendix

Sample Student Research Papers

We chose these student examples to represent the results of shorter research assignments. As we note several times throughout this book, there is no one correct way to approach research and writing, although these papers follow processes similar to those we describe and adhere to appropriate citation formats—one MLA, the other APA.

Of course, the nature of your assignment(s) may well be very different from these, but perhaps these students' work will help you to react to decisions you assume the writers made about sources, the order of presentation, the central arguments, support for the arguments, word choices, and stylistic considerations.

As you read, consider the following questions and prepare to discuss your responses with your classmates after you complete your reading and analysis of the papers. For each:

What is the writer's central argument—the writer's thesis? How is it conveyed? What might you have done differently—or not? How is the thesis supported? What are the supporting arguments?

In what ways is the writer able to establish ethos? Consider other forms of persuasion. Does the writer employ logos, for instance, to support arguments? How so?

Be mindful of the ways in which the writer integrates sources. Paying special attention to instances of summary, paraphrase, and direct quotation, how might you comment on the integration of source materials and the sources the writer chose?

Consider working backward in analyzing this paper. That is, create a rough outline or anti-outline, as we've called it, attempting to discern the writer's process. What is the result? How does the paper seem to have been effectively constructed? How might it have been improved?

Comment on the writer's style and use of language. What, if anything, would you change?

Review the writer's citation formats and bibliography. Which citation format does the writer appear to use? How accurate are the citations and use of this particular format?

In fact, what is your overall assessment of the choices you can infer the writer made and their effects?

Sample Student Essay: MLA

Nadezh Mayo
Media Central College
Gold-Diggers and Vamps: Sexuality, Race, and Class in the Court
Case *Rhinelander v. Rhinelander*

On November 9, 1925, Leonard Kip Rhinelander, a wealthy member of the social elite from a well-regarded New York family, took his wife to court in an attempt to annul their marriage. Alice Rhinelander, born Alice Jones, fought the annulment, as newspapers and tabloids across America made a spectator sport of the emotional proceedings that unfolded over the next year. The seemingly happy couple, who had written many romantic letters during the three years of their courtship, hit a roadblock in their new marriage when a New York newspaper published a story claiming that Alice was the daughter of a "colored man." According to American ideas about race in the 1920s, that meant that Alice was black as well. Alice also worked as a nanny, and a scandal emerged when it became known that a famous Rhinelander had married a black servant girl. Although Leonard at first swore that he would stand by Alice no matter what the papers said and no matter her race, he soon changed his mind. One year after their marriage, Leonard and Alice found themselves the central figures in the New York state court case *Rhinelander v. Rhinelander*.

At the trial Leonard claimed that Alice had defrauded him by misrepresenting herself as white, and that he would never have married her if her had known that she had "colored blood" in her (Onwuachi-Willig 2401).

> Note how the writer piques the reader's interest with contextual information that leads to the central argument.

This particular case seems to have disappeared from popular accounts of history. It was not a Supreme Court case, and it is not as well-known as other cases pertaining to racial restrictions on marriage. (In fact, only two lawyers are known to have had access to the full court transcripts [2401].) For example, many people have heard of the case, *Loving v. Virginia*, in which an interracial couple from Virginia fought for the right to be together in 1967 and won, legalizing interracial marriage throughout the United States. The case of *Rhinelander v. Rhinelander* may not be as well known, but the trial is an equally important snapshot in American history. The court proceedings express American conceptions of race in the 1920s, as well as American ideas about the roles of men, women, and sexual boundaries in the context of race. To describe the trial as an attack on inter racial marriage and the "pollution" of the white race by blacks is not wrong, but it is incomplete. Upon closer examination, the court case *Rhinelander v. Rhinelander*, although fought on the grounds of racial fraud, in fact has as much to do with sexuality and gender as it does with race. Indeed, it is nearly

> The writer has given enough context to present her thesis statement, the central argument of her paper.

impossible to think about the *Rhinelander* case without addressing the important interactions of race, sexuality, and class in public perceptions of Alice—a poor, black woman.

The most immediate example of the role of sexuality in the *Rhinelander* case is Alice's reputation as a "vamp." Leonard's lawyer spent much of his energy trying to convince America that Alice was a sexual predator who had duped Leonard into marriage. The vamp was a popular female archetype of the 1920s. According to historians Earl Lewis and Heidi Ardizzone, ". . . the female vamp was overtly sexual and always dangerous. . . . she did deprive them [men] of their power and the predatory role of their social privilege. Men, not women, were expected to be the sexual aggressors" (Lewis and Ardizzone 56). The image of the vamp was not associated with women of color in particular, but there is certainly a connection between commonly held beliefs about black, or partially black, women and the vamp. Women who were of both white and black heritage, like Alice, were referred to a "mulatto." Mulatto women were depicted as psychologically troubled. "The female version of the tragic mulatto . . . accentuated her sexual beauty" and had a "desire to gain power, wealth, or whiteness by sleeping with white men" (29). The fact that mulatto women were seen as sexual gold diggers with a manipulative streak explains why it was so easy for Leonard's lawyer to convince the jury and the public to view Alice as a vamp.

Notice the writer's appropriate use of MLA in-text citation.

Alice's letters often contained references to sexual attraction or sexual activity between herself and Leonard. She wrote one such letter on November 17, 1921:

Listen Lenard [*sic*], I have had some sweet hearts, but I have not loved them, like I have taken to you so. I have never let a fellow love and caress me, the way you do Lenard, because you make me feel so happy, and loyable [*sic*] toward you dear. But would it be awful if you had me my self alone. What you would not do to me. I can imagine. (Lewis and Ardizzone 89)

Another of Alice's letters, from May 19, 1922, reads, "I got undressed and got into bed which you can see me in bed like the Antoinette [Marie Antoinette], and snuggled in bed.

And read all of your letters, but you made me feel very passionate for the want of you, telling me how happy my little hand as often made you feel, and several other things, but can't help to tell you"

(Onwuachi-Willig 2436). By expressing her sexuality, Alice showed herself to be a vamp in the eyes of Mills and the public. The sexual content of her letters classified her as sexually promiscuous, despite the fact that the letters were shared intimately between Leonard and Alice alone.

Leonard's letters were just as sexual as Alice's—more so, in fact, based on all the letters I have found. In July of 1922 he wrote, "Oh, Sweetheart, many, many nights, when I lay in bed and think about my darling girl, it [his penis] acts the very same way and longs for your warm body to crawl upon me, take it in your soft, smooth hands, and then work it up very slowly between your open legs" (Onwuachi-Willig 2433). One month earlier, in June of 1922, Leonard sent an even more explicit letter to Alice:

> Do you ever think, when you are lying in bed at night, how I used to make you passionate with my warm lips, and the way I did it? . . . Do you remember, honeybunch, how I used to put my head between your legs and how I used to caress you with my lips and tongue? . . . Oh! I often think when I used to lift up your night-gown and crawl down to the foot of the bed, so as I could be right under you. "Please, dear, come." Do you recall how I asked you to do that. (Smith-Pryor 153)

Compared to the detailed descriptions of Leonard's language, the suggested imaginings of Alice's letters are downright tame.

Yet only Alice was deemed sexually deviant for engaging in such talk. The discussion of Alice's status as a vamp in the courtroom and in the newspapers and tabloids shows how society attempted to police Alice's sexuality. The sexual content of Alice's letters served as more than a window into her sex life; it was meant to illuminate her character. Leonard's lawyer, Isaac Mills, painted Alice as a calculating, devious woman who preyed on Leonard's innocence (Lewis and Ardizzone 53). Because she had a sexual relationship with Leonard, the assumption was that she must also have been manipulative and a gold-digger, like the popular image of the mulatto woman. Alice's sexual activities dictated how every other aspect of her character was viewed. Many newspapers and tabloids echoed Mills's accusations about Alice's self-serving motivations behind her relationship with Leonard.

Perhaps surprisingly, Alice won the trial. The jury's decision to side with Alice and against Leonard is an expression of societal views on proper social conduct and racial roles. One way to read the outcome of the trial is that Leonard needed to be "punished" for his transgression of publically committing to Alice and cementing his relationship with her through marriage. And punished he was: After losing the trial, he was disinherited financially (although not emotionally) by his father, and died single at the age of thirty-four, "reportedly of a broken heart" (Onwuachi-Willig 2456). It may be said that in winning the jury's vote, Alice was rewarded for conforming the stereotype of a working-class black woman. For Leonard, a wealthy, white man, falling for Alice, who was poor and black, was scandalous in 1920s New York. Alice, though, did exactly what was expected of her. Society saw young black women as sexually indiscriminate and manipulative. Whether or not these words accurately describe Alice's actions, the allegation of being a vamp was brought against her in trial and in the media time and again. Like all poor black women of her time, the public already viewed her as a vamp even before her name appeared in the newspaper, by virtue of her race and class. While Leonard defied everyone's expectations of him as a wealthy, white gentlemen, Alice *confirmed* the expectations that the jury already had of her. Leonard betrayed his social position by marrying Alice, but Alice could hardly be faulted for acting according to her nature. In effect, Alice was rewarded for upholding the stereotype of black women as treacherous sexual vixens. Viewed through this lens, the trial's outcome—which at first glance may appear to have been a victory for the black community—was in fact both racist and sexist in its supporting conventional ideologies.

In light of Leonard's punishment for his relationship with Alice, it may appear that Leonard's sexuality was policed just in the way

Alice's was. In reality, however, it was not Leonard's sexuality that was being policed, but something else entirely. Leonard was not attacked for his decision to have a sexual relationship with Alice; he was attacked for choosing to marry her even after learning that she was not entirely white. It was not acceptable for Alice to have a sexual relationship with Leonard before getting married. Once it was revealed in court that she had slept with him, every aspect of her character was called into question as a result. Her decision to have sex with Leonard introduced the possibility that she was a lying, selfish slut (to her detractors) who cared more about money than she cared about Leonard. At the same time, it *was* socially acceptable for Leonard to sleep with Alice outside the bounds of marriage. Premarital sex did not leave the same mark upon Leonard's character as it did on Alice's. Sex, for a man, is not viewed a *loss* of virginity the way it is for a woman, but a *gain* in masculinity and experience. Psychologists Michael J. Marks and R. Chris Fraley point out that the sexual double standard between men and women has long existed in Western societies, and that women are judged more harshly than men for having many partners (Marks and Fraley 20). Although Leonard's having sex with Alice without any specific plan to marry her was not exactly a source of conventional approval, it was not enough to destroy his character. As a man, and a white man at that, it was believed, if quietly so, that Leonard had an inherent right to sex that Alice was denied.

Leonard had a right to marriage as well as sex, but he threw that right away when he decided to waste (in conventional view) his social position on Alice. Leonard's choice in sexual practices did, in fact, come under attack: Lee Parsons Davis, Alice's lawyer, read a letter written by Leonard. This letter, referenced earlier in this paper, describes the act of performing oral sex on a woman, which Davis deems "an unnatural thing" (Smith-Pryor 154). However, although oral sex was frowned upon, Leonard's decision to engage in sexual activity of one form or another did not come under attack. It was entering the socially approved institution of marriage with Alice—not engaging in the taboo activity of premarital of sex—that sullied Leonard's good name. Indeed, many white men throughout history have engaged in sexual activity with black women. There are many examples of (often nonconsensual) sexual activity between male slave masters and their female slaves (Sonnen). As was the case for the men who came before him, it was acceptable for Leonard to have sex with Alice but it was not acceptable for him to validate their relationship through marriage. It was marrying Alice while presumably knowing about her racial background that posed a threat to Leonard's social status.

Sexuality factored into the *Rhinelander* case once again when Alice's lawyer, Davis, implied that a man could not be sexually assaulted by a woman. Davis joked dismissively that the accusations against Alice were "'. . . the first time I ever heard of a girl criminally assaulting a man'" (Lewis and Ardizzone 67). The question here is not the purpose behind his argument, but rather the idea that Davis put forth and the receptiveness of the jury to this idea. By siding with Alice, the jury showed that they most likely

> Note that the writer integrates direct quotes with paraphrase, always citing appropriately.

agreed with Davis's proposition that a woman cannot sexually assault a man. In Davis's eyes the thought of such a thing happening was not only laughable but also impossible. Regardless of whether Leonard and Alice Rhinelander's relationship involved any form of sexual assault perpetrated by either partner, the argument is a noteworthy one. This argument assumes that male and female sexuality, sexual practices, and potential sexual crimes are dictated by sex and gender alone; it presents the idea that a woman cannot be sexually aggressive and that a man cannot be a victim of sexual crime. Although it is possible for a woman to assault a man, and it does happen, this false belief still affects how we think about sexual assault today, and it helps to maintain the stigma against male victims of sexual assault (Pappas).

In what Lewis and Ardizzone refer to as "arguably the most memorable and troubling point in a trial already filled with drama and emotion" (Lewis and Ardizzone 156), Alice was asked to disrobe in court, baring her back, breasts, and legs for the jury and judge. Alice reportedly wept and had to be physically supported by her mother as she bared her naked body; later, she was so distraught that her father carried her out of the building. The purpose of the display, according to her lawyer, was to illustrate to the jury that Alice's body showed her obvious blackness and that therefore Leonard must have known that Alice was black before marrying her. Alice was humiliated in court—and in the countless retellings and visual reconstructions that followed—at the request of her own attorney, her advocate.

Relevant to this case is the charged racial and sexual past behind the public nudity of black women. The image of Alice's naked body

> Here is an example of the writer's having successfully introduced a longer quote, which is set off and in-dented from the body of the paper.

... reverberates through a violent racial history and flickers with the remem-brances of a multitude of atrocious vignettes: enslaved men and women standing on auction blocks, stripped before the examina-tion of prospective purchasers; the icon of a half-dressed woman in chains on her knees pleading to her white abolitionist "sister" for help; the "Hottentot Venus," a southern African woman named Sara Baartman, brought to England and put on display, usually nude, for scientific and curiosity-seeking audiences. . . . (Lewis and Ardizzone 156)

Alice was humiliated in a way that would never be inflicted upon a white woman; the fact that the court and public spectators already viewed Alice as black, and therefore inferior, allowed them to justify treating her in such a way. In the context of a long history of sexual deg-radation and public humiliation of black women, Alice's blackness in the eyes of her spectators made such a bodily display an acceptable course of action. Alice was part of a long line of African American women "asked or forced to bare her body to satisfy the needs and curiosities of white men" (Lewis and Ardizzone 157). Alice's treatment in this incident shows that the court already had a firm view of Alice as a sexual object.

Although the incident was private (no reporters were present), descriptions promptly appeared in the newspapers, including both fact-based retellings and vivid, dramatic imaginings. Many papers produced recreations of the scene in the form of sketches that depicted Alice partially naked. The *Evening Graphic*, however, outdid all other new sources when it published a photograph of the scene; the tabloid hired a model to pose as Alice, and then cut and pasted the image together with pictures from the actual trial. The composite photograph resulted in a highly sexualized—even pornographic—version of the event:

> The *Graphic*'s so-called composograph featured a half-nude Alice
> Rhinelander in front of her husband, the lawyers, the judge, and
> her mother with the caption, "Alice disrobes in Court to Keep
> Her Husband." Not surprisingly for the *Graphic* (referred to by
> its critics as the *Pornographic*), the paper sexualized the scene
> when it showed Alice in a scanty slip instead of the lowered coat
> described by the court stenographer. (Smith-Pryor 204)

Alice's emotional and painful ordeal was distorted for the pleasure—sexual and otherwise—of the viewing public. Her story was told, retold, and extravagantly embellished for the fulfillment of onlookers, with little concern for Alice as a person. In the eyes of feminist writers Catharine MacKinnon and Andrea Dworkin, "objectification involves treating a person, someone with humanity, as an object of merely instrumental worth, and consequently reducing this person to the status of an object for use. The objectified individual is made into a tool for others' sexual purposes. Objectification, therefore, constitutes a serious harm to a person's humanity" (Papadaki). The tabloid obsession with discussing and recreating Alice's nudity devalued her humanity and focused all attention on her physical body alone; Alice was turned into an object to be played with, enjoyed, fantasized about, and tossed aside. It is important to note that, with the exception of her mother, Alice undressed in a room full of male spectators (for the judge, lawyers, jury, and stenographer were all men). This part of the trial reinforces then-socially acceptable expressions of male and female sexuality, in which men act and women are acted upon.

One way to view the disrobing debacle is as an indirect punishment for Alice. This is, of course, simply one view of many, but it is certainly worth considering how Alice's actions may have justified, in the eyes of her spectators, the unjust treatment that she suffered. The incident seems like an indirect punishment for metaphorically and physically baring all in front of Leonard and expressing her sexual urges to him in her letters. To reiterate, Alice was not passive in her relationship with Leonard. Just as Leonard was punished for committing to Alice—his racial and social inferior—Alice too was punished for failing to conform to societal expectations of her sexual conduct.

In one letter, Alice writes, "Len do you remember in old Marie Antoinette the good times we have had and now look how we after [*sic*] suffer for it. Do you remember how you loved to chase me around" (Lewis and Ardizzone 98). In another letter to Leonard dated February 9, 1921, Alice writes,

> Just think of me, this evening being hear alone, mother and father and sister . . . as gone to the Westchester. . . . And I am hear alone, thinking of you, dear heart. I said to myself when they were going out, of the front door. I only wished Lenard was coming down this evening. How I could caress, you dear. . . . I went to bed, and stayed in my room, until five minutes to twelve, and got in bed, at twenty-five after I hopped in bed, and laid there, thinking of you, dear heart [*sic*]. (Lewis and Ardizzone 90)

Although both would be considered tame by modern standards, each of the excerpts above alludes to a shared sex life between Alice and Leonard. She feels comfortable referring to sex they had in the Marie Antoinette Hotel. Alice writes Leonard that she thinks of him when she is in bed and wishes to be alone with him in her home—the implication being for sexual reasons. In a third letter, Alice writes, "But would it be awful if you had me my self alone. What you would not do to me. I can imagine . . ." (Lewis and Ardizzone 89). This letter further demonstrates that Alice receives pleasure from fantasizing about sexual contact with Leonard.

Clearly, Alice was open about her sexuality. Upon hearing the letters written between the two, the spectators of the trial could not pretend that female sexuality did not exist. Alice broke social guidelines by openly addressing her sexual desires and needs; even worse, those private desires became public for all the world to see, whether she wanted that or not. Sexually, Alice was an equal to her husband, rather

> The writer is generally successful in providing transitional words and phrases to link ideas—or to contrast ideas—logically and as signposts to the reader.

than a subordinate, as was socially expected of her. In the 1920s, "[c]ommentators and social analysts still held that only unrespectable girls expressed themselves sexually outside the bounds of marriage. Love led to marriage, which provided the reason for sex. Women who had sex outside of marriage were perceived as somehow delinquent and the victims of their own desires" (Lewis and Ardizzone 147–148). In a sense, Alice had too much power. She was too much an equal participant in her sexual relationship with Leonard and was too comfortable with her own sexuality—and independent female sexuality was a frightening concept for many onlookers of the Rhinelander trial. Consciously or unconsciously, the balance needed to be restored to reassure onlookers that the social order was being maintained. By watching Alice undress, they stripped her of the power that she had in her relationship with Leonard, making her once again the acted upon, rather than the actor in her sexual life. Further, the trial reinforced the unfortunate stereotype of the degeneracy of the black woman.

Ultimately, *Rhinelander v. Rhinelander* had a lot to say about the proper roles of women, and specifically working-class black women. These three categories are intricately

> Notice the ways in which the writer summarizes—reiterates, but does not merely repeat—the central argument of the paper.

intertwined, and they are nearly impossible to separate. What is means to be a black woman is distinct from what it means to be simply be black, or to be a woman. Black women occupy a unique social position in which their race informs what society believes to be true about their womanhood and sexuality, and in which their sexuality affects their socially perceived level of "blackness." This case has as much to do with the proper sexual and romantic roles of men and women as it does with the roles of whites and blacks. Ultimately, the case exemplifies prevailing—and not completely resolved—stereotypes and attitudes about privilege, the underclass, race, and gender.

Works Cited

The Works Cited demonstrates appropriate use of the MLA citation format.

Lewis, Earl, and Heidi Ardizzone. *Love on Trial: An American Scandal in Black and White*. W. W. Norton, 2001.

Marks, Michael J., and R. Chris Fraley. "Confirmation Bias and the Sexual Double Standard." *Sex Roles*, vol. 54, no. 1–2, 2006, pp. 19–26.

Onwuachi-Willig, Angela. "A Beautiful Lie: Exploring Rhinelader v. Rhinelander as a Formative Lesson on Race, Identity, Marriage, and Family." *California Law Review*, vol. 95, no. 6, Dec. 2007, pp. 2393–458.

Papadaki, Evangelia. "Feminist Perspectives on Objectification." *The Stanford Encyclopedia of Philosophy*, Fall 2011, 22 Apr. 2012, plato.stanford.edu/entries/feminism-objectification/.

Pappas, Stephanie. "Male Victims of Sexual Abuse Face Unique Challenges." *Live Science*, Tech Media Network, 17 Feb. 2011, www.livescience.com/12909-senator-scott-brown-male-sexual-abuse-stigma.html.

Smith-Pryor, Elizabeth M. *Property Rites: The Rhinelander Trial, Passing, and the Protection of Whiteness*. U of North Carolina, 2009.

Sonnen, Gloria. "Master-Slave Relationships." *The Enslaved American Woman: Her Unique Plight*, Bowdoin College, 12 Apr. 2000, www.bowdoin.edu/~prael/projects/gsonnen/page4.html.

Sample Student Essay: APA

George Bate

Oakton Community College

The Relationship Between Economics and Motivation in
Coordination with Complex Theories of Motivation

Psychologists throughout history have attempted to define and recognize the reasoning
behind the actions and behavior of human beings. However, many of the proposed theories
often conflict with or directly contradict one
another (Huitt, 2011). Furthermore, such theories are often singular in nature and fail to
address an individual's collective motivation.

> Notice that the title of this paper—reflecting its social science content—contrasts with the type of title presented in the first paper. The differences among disciplines are often reflected in the nature of the titles of research-oriented articles or papers.

Several theories proposed, specifically Abraham Maslow's Hierarchy of
Needs, introduce the concept of motivation for financial needs once an
individual's basic needs are satisfied (Maslow, 1943). This article initially
explores and analyzes the various, often conflict-
ing theories of motivation and then examines
the distinct correlation between an individual's
motivation and money[1]. This is briefly illustrated
for modern, economically stable individuals,
who recognize money as an important, often
vital motivator. Once such key theories are de-

> On this page and elsewhere, the writer effectively uses explanatory footnotes to add contextual information that doesn't need to be in the body of the paper but that is helpful and informational to the reader.

fined and analyzed, the relationship between economics and motivation will be demonstrated through a variety of analytical, data-driven

---

[1]Money, defined within the context of this article, pertains to an individual's earn-
ings. In other words, a discussion on the correlation between money and motivation
pertains to an individual's motivation to earn money or obtain wealth.

and opinionated means that offer different conclusions regarding such a correlation.

Keywords: Motivation, Maslow's Hierarchy of Needs, basic needs

Dr. Richard W. Scholl (2002) of the University of Rhode Island stated, "Motivation is goal directed, that is, individual motivation can best be explained in terms of an individual's attempt to achieve certain personal goals" (Huitt, 2002). In simplified terms, motivation is defined by the Merriam-Webster dictionary as "the act or process of giving someone a reason for doing something" ("Motivation-Definition," n.d.). Sigmund Freud introduced a psychological perspective on this concept as early as the 1890s. Freud, who was eventually known as the "father of psychoanalysis," introduced complex psychological concepts, such as the unconscious mind, the id/ego/super-ego and the life and death instincts (Rana, 1997). Specifically, his theories of life and death instincts addressed individuals' motivations by explaining that people are driven to act in certain ways to satisfy two basic needs (Gollwitzer & Oettingen, 2001, p. 10110). Freud enforced the concept that instincts "are the principal motivating forces in the mental realm" and that, subsequently, people have two conflicting desires (Thornton, n.d.). These distinct, central desires are life and death—life in that people are intrinsically driven to survive and satisfy their biological needs and death in that people are motivated to act in aggressive, cruel and often self-destructive ways (Thornton, n.d.). While Freud's initial theories of motivation are often disputed in the modern age, the concepts he introduced were used as the basis of subsequent theories that further defined an individual's conflicting motivations. Some of these theories introduce the concept of a

> Notice the writer's concise introduction, giving the reader central concepts that are important to understanding his argument, which is expressed clearly.

173

correlation between motivation and economics, which is specifically explored in Maslow's Hierarchy of Needs. This paper will explore this relationship.

Initial Examination of Complex Theories of Motivation

Following the proposed theories of William McDougall in 1932 and Henry Murray in 1938,[2] Abraham Maslow introduced a theory of motivation that shaped the course of the entire field (Gollwitzer & Oettingen, 2001, p. 10110). Expanding upon Freud's teachings, Maslow introduced a "Hierarchy of Needs" in 1943 that outlined motivations based on echelons in which initial needs must be satisfied before advancing up the pyramid (Maslow, 1943). Maslow's humanistic theory stated that each lower level on his pyramid "must be met before moving to the next higher level" (Huitt, 2011). The first level was defined as physiological; People have a deep, intrinsic desire to satisfy their biological needs, such as hunger or thirst. Once satisfying these needs, people are driven to obtain safety and security, which includes safety from danger and financial security. The third level is a feeling of belonging and love, as people now feel a desire to develop healthy relationships and feel accepted by their peers once the first two levels are met. The fourth level involves esteem in that individuals feel the need to achieve their goals and gain approval or recognition. After progressing from this level, people attempt to satisfy deep, cognitive needs, such as to explore and understand the world as it is. Aesthetics are often associated with this level, as people attempt to achieve order and beauty in their lives. This level is also associated with cognitive needs.[3] The final steps are grouped together and involve

---

[2]McDougall expanded upon Freud's theories by defining, not two, but sixteen basic instincts that motivate human beings. Six years later, Murray introduced "20 psychogenic needs," such as the need for nurturance or the need of succorance (Gollwitzer & Oettingen, 2001, p. 10110).

[3]Cognitive needs are defined as desires that structure aspects of life into meaningful categories (Huitt, 2011).

self-actualization and then transcendence; this level involves realizing one's true, inner potential and then helping others find self-fulfillment. Maslow believed this final step was the ultimate motivational factor that only a select group of people will ever achieve (Huitt, 2011). Many psychologists were fascinated by Maslow's teachings and have since analyzed and expanded upon his theories to perfect a theory of motivation.

While Maslow's "Hierarchy of Needs" is an absolute examination into the motivation of individuals, other theories are distinct and do not address overlapping motivators. Humanistic theories of motivation, famously "illustrated in Maslow's Hierarchy of Needs," highlight the "strong cognitive reasons to perform actions" (Cherry, "Theories of Motivation"). The four other main theories are specific and do not offer an in depth analysis of all aspects of life. This is illustrated by the Instinct Theory of Motivation, which states people behave in certain ways, because they are "evolutionarily programmed to do so" (Cherry, "Theories of Motivation"). People are driven by a variety of human instincts, such as attachment, shame and anger (Cherry, "Theories of Motivation"). However, this approach exclusively addresses one motivator and fails to describe others.

> As you will see as you read the bibliography, the writer indicates that there are no page numbers for this information. Moreover, he cites several works by this author; therefore, he must include the title so that the reader knows to which source the writer is referring.

Another singular approach is the "Incentive Theory of Motivation." This theory states that external rewards motivate people to act in certain ways. Psychological concepts, such as reinforcement and attachment,[4] play a role in the understanding of this theory. Similar to the "Instinct Theory," the "Incentive Theory" addresses only a single motivator, in this

---

[4]Within his theories on Operant Conditioning, B.F. Skinner introduced the concept of reinforcement (McLeod, 2007). He defined reinforcement as anything "that increases the likelihood that a response will occur" (Cherry, "What is Reinforcement?"). Attachment involves "a deep and enduring emotional bond that connects one person to another across time and space," as defined by psychologists Mary Ainsworth and John Bowlby (McLeod, 2009).

case external rewards, and overlooks the influences of other factors. Additionally, this singular theme is seen in the Drive Theory of Motivation, which states people are motivated to act in a certain manner in order to "reduce the internal tension that is caused by unmet needs" (Cherry, "Theories of Motivation"). For example, an individual would drink water in order to reduce their thirst. This theory explains how human biology motivates individuals to behave and act. However, critics have deemed this theory untrue or invalid. Critics have suggested, for example, that some people eat when they are not hungry and are, therefore, not attempting to satisfy an internal need (Cherry, "Theories of Motivation").

The "Arousal Theory of Motivation" is also singular in nature, but has faced similar criticism. This theory suggests that people act in certain ways to "decrease or increase levels of arousal" (Cherry, "Theories of Motivation"). For example, when one is experiencing a state of low arousal, they might decide to go to the gym or watch a movie. However, if one is highly aroused, he or she might relax or read a book. The conclusion of this theory, that people are motivated to constantly "maintain an optimal state of arousal," has been disputed by critics (Cherry, "Theories of Motivation").

Collective Analysis of Conflicting Theories

Intrinsic or extrinsic theories of motivation, as displayed in the previous section, all attempt to answer the question: Why do human beings act the way they do? (Chamorro-Premuzic, 2013). Despite having differing, often conflicting theories of motivation, most psychologists agree on the importance of motivation. Psychologists question whether changes in human behavior are determined by "environmental/ecological" influences, such as our memory, emotions or biology, or by an individual's life experiences (Huitt, 2011).

> This is a very good transitional paragraph for the writer's argument and as a guidepost for the reader.

> This is another example of where, ideally, there should be a page reference; however, the website from which this article was retrieved apparently offers no such guidance.

It is important to note that the theories previously described might be singular in their analysis, but must be understood as a whole. They all attempt to answer the key questions regarding motivation. All the theories must be considered as one entity to entirely understand the concept of motivation, which is why Maslow's Hierarchy of Needs is still relevant and influential as it addresses *all* aspects of human motivation (Čížek, 2012, p. 4). For example, the "Instinct Theory of Motivation" only addresses human evolution's influences on human behavior (Cherry, "Theories of Motivation"). It specifically ignores the influences of other factors, such as external rewards, emotions and life experiences. Conversely, Maslow's "Hierarchy of Needs" addresses aspects of, not only the "Instinct Theory of Motivation," but also aspects of the "Incentive Theory," "Drive Theory." and "Arousal Theory," among many others (Maslow, 1943). W. Huitt (2011) elaborated on the overlapping nature of some of the aforementioned theories, but Huitt recognizes that most are very distinct and do not cover the same material (Huitt, 2011). Interestingly, if Maslow's "Hierarchy of Needs" is considered in a practical sense, a distinct correlation between economics and motivation can be recognized.

Economics and Motivation in Coordination With Maslow's Hierarchy of Needs

If considered as a collective entity, similar to Maslow's "Hierarchy of Needs," the aforementioned theories holistically offer an in-depth analysis of what motivates people. Through his "Hierarchy of Needs," Abraham Maslow recognizes that basic needs must be met before advancing to higher levels of motivation (Maslow, 1943). However, for economically stable individuals, basic needs are automatically satisfied. This supports the concept that motivation is dependent on the person and her or his situation, as exemplified by Petr Čížek (2012, p. 49). In "The Application Of Maslow's Hierarchy of Needs to the

-Entrepreneur's Motivation—The Example From Region Pardubice," Dr. Čížek offers a practical analysis of Maslow's "Hierarchy of Needs" within the entrepreneurial and working realm. Dr. Čížek further explores the relationship between money and motivation when he states, "It is also concluded that money related motivation factors are very strong among the entrepreneurs, however [the] majority of the respondents refused to sacrifice their time with family to obtain higher financial income" (Čížek, 2012, p. 1). This practical demonstration of Maslow's teachings highlights that, for economically stable individuals such as entrepreneurs, basic needs are rarely addressed. Instead, such entrepreneurs are "highly self-motivated, amounting almost to an irresistible urge to succeed in their economic goals" (Čížek, 2012, p. 2). For this group of people, money is a leading motivator that takes precedence over nearly all other aspects of life.

Dr. Čížek explores another concept: that once the initial levels of Maslow's "Hierarchy of Needs" are achieved, "higher needs don't have such strict hierarchy of motivation" (Čížek, 2012, p. 49). This is demonstrated by the entrepreneurs' sheer will to achieve economic success on their own. This aspect of entrepreneurship shows that "one of the main motivators is self actualization" (Čížek, 2012, p. 2). In this sense, Dr. Čížek is establishing a correlation between money and different levels of motivation, as initially defined by Abraham

> Notice how the writer successfully integrates his sources with his commentary and summation of previous information

Maslow. Obtaining wealth is a complex concept that often transcends Maslow's Hierarchy of Needs, as it is related to a variety of his defined levels. People will attempt to obtain wealth in order to feel financially secure, as demonstrated on level two of Maslow's Hierarchy (Huitt, 2011). However, Dr. Čížek also demonstrates that money is related to more advanced levels of motivation, such as self-actualization and transcendence as many economically stable individuals experience self-fulfillment through their pursuit of wealth (Čížek, 2012, p. 2, p. 49).

Correlation Between Economics and Motivation as Demonstrated by the Tension Between Intrinsic and Extrinsic Motivation

As prelude to further discussion of the relationship between economics and motivation, intrinsic and extrinsic motivation must be defined within the context of this study. Extrinsic motivation occurs when people are motivated to "perform a behavior or engage in an activity in order to earn a reward or avoid a punishment" (Cherry, "Difference Between Extrinsic and

> The writer effectively explains the need to introduce another complex concept as he continues to support his central argument.

Intrinsic Motivation") Extrinsic motivation can be seen, for example, when a student studies to receive a good grade or works a part time job for a financial reward. Conversely, intrinsic motivation "involves engaging in a behavior because it is personally rewarding..." (Cherry, "Difference Between Extrinsic . . .") For example, a person exhibits intrinsic motivation if they play a sport for personal enjoyment or if they play a game because it is exciting (Cherry, Difference Between Extrinsic"). Within the context of this article, extrinsic motivation is associated with financial rewards or economics.

> This is a good, logical link to the earlier parts of this paper.

A relationship between money and motivation is shown through an examination into the balance between intrinsic and extrinsic rewards. In his article in the *Harvard Business Review*, Tomas Chamorro-Premuzic attempts to answer the question, "Does Money Really Affect Motivation?" Chamorro-Premuzic describes a state of tension that is naturally created between extrinsic and intrinsic motives. He introduces the idea that a person's extrinsic and intrinsic motivations are constantly conflicting with one another. He states, "[f]inancial rewards can ultimately depress or 'crowd out' intrinsic goals (e.g., enjoyment, sheer curiosity, learning or personal challenge)" (Chamorro-Premuzic, 2012). In this sense, extrinsic motivation can be associated with financial rewards, while intrinsic motivation involves personal gratification.

This specific correlation between money and motivation is shown through a meta-analysis conducted by Edward L. Deci, Richard Koestner and Richard M. Ryan. The professors used 128 controlled experiments to highlight the "effects of extrinsic rewards on intrinsic motivation" (Deci, Koestner, & Ryan, 1999, p. 1). Using a variety of diverse variables, from marshmallows to dollars, the professors concluded that external incentives have negative effects on intrinsic motivation. Furthermore, external rewards, specifically money, often combat or overrule one's intrinsic motivation (Deci, Koestner, & Ryan, 1999, p. 27). In other terms, "[w]hen rewards are tangible and foreseeable (if subjects know in advance how much extra money they will receive) intrinsic motivation decreases by 36%" (Chamorro-Premuzic, 2013). This highlights another complexity of the relationship between money and motivation, as extrinsic motivation often overrules intrinsic motivation; individuals experience overwhelming incentives to obtain wealth, rather than to achieve internal gratification. This relationship can also be seen in a practical sense through an examination of how money motivates in the workplace.

> This is another example of the writer's effective way of transitioning between ideas.

Motivation of Money in the Workplace

Money and motivation are highly correlated, as exemplified by the ways in which workers are motivated. The perceived general basis of all work spawns from the desire to obtain wealth. Chuck Leddy of the Harvard Gazette examines this concept and similarly attempts to explain how money motivates people by answering the question, "Do employees work harder for higher pay?" (Leddy, 2013). Leddy recounts the research of Harvard Business School professor Deepak Malhotra and two of his Harvard colleagues Duncan Gilchrist and Michael Luca. Dr. Malhotra noted that previous research indicated that "paying people more than they expect may elicit reciprocity in the form of greater effort or productivity" (Leddy, 2013). However, Dr. Malhotra's research was indicative of a slightly altered conclusion:

Dr. Malhotra and his colleagues conducted a field study with 266 workers. These 266 workers were divided into three groups. One group was given three dollars for every hour of work, another group was given four dollars an hour and the third group began with three dollars and then received a surprise one dollar pay grade to match the highest group. The results indicated that the third group had the best performance in a variety of workplace activities. Dr. Malhotra concluded that non-monetary incentives "can be powerful motivators," but that money is still a leading motivator. He also concluded that it is not just *what* you are paid that influences your motivation, and therefore performance, but also *how* you are paid (Leddy, 2013).

Sara L. Rynes, Barry Gerhart, and Kathleen A. Minette (2004) of the University of Tennessee at Martin similarly concluded that "Money is not the only motivator and it is not the primary motivator for everyone. However, there is overwhelming evidence that money is an important motivator for most people" (Rynes, Gerhart, & Minette, 2004, p. 12). This further illustrates a distinct relationship between economics and motivation and highlights to what degree wealth influences the average person.

> The writer effectively summarizes very complex information in this section

Discussion

As the research presented illustrates, a distinct relationship between money and motivation exists. While some psychologists offer varying opinions on the matter, it is important to note than most research indicates that money is a leading motivator, especially for economically stable individuals who have previously satisfied their basic needs. From a practical standpoint, this correlation between money and motivation is truly shown in the workplace. Workers will constantly attempt to achieve their financial goals, as indicated through a variety of workplace motivational theories. For example, Herzberg's "Two-Factor or Motivator-Hygiene" theory states that workers are motivated by hygiene and motivator—hygiene, as in salary and benefits and motivator, as in recognition and responsibility. Other workplace motivational theories similarly explore the relationship between money and motivation, such as the "Goals and Objectives as Motivation Theory"[5] (Fisher, 2009). Once the lower levels of Maslow's "Hierarchy of Needs" are achieved, money becomes paramount. Obtaining wealth is a key motivator that plays a part in many of the upper levels of Maslow's "Hierarchy of Needs."

Critics of money's influence on motivation might point to the precedence other motivations take over money. However, research provides validity to the claim that money is a key motivator. Sara L. Rynes, Barry Gerhart, and Kathleen A. Minette (2004) discussed money as a motivator for workers and stated, ". . . [W]hile managers will (and should) consider both financial and nonfinancial tools for attracting, motivating, and retaining employees, it would be a mistake to conclude, based

> In the start of this paragraph, the writer acknowledges the potential of a reader's objections to his arguments and the theories he presents, an effective way to reinforce the desirability of his own argument.

on general surveys, that monetary rewards are not highly important" (Rynes, Gerhart, & Minette, 2004, p. 12). As obtaining wealth is a key determinant in the direction of individuals' lives, it is important to note the decided influence of economics vis-à-vis motivation.

References

Chamorro-Premuzic, T. (2013, April 10). Does money really affect motivation? A review of the research. Retrieved from https://hbr.org/2013/04/does-money-really-affect-motiv

---

[5] In her article "Motivation and Leadership in Social Work Management: A Review of Theories and Related Studies Motivation and Leadership in Social Work Administration," Dr. Elizabeth A. Fisher of Shippensburg University explores these workplace, theories of motivation. The Goals and Objectives as Motivation Theory states that "[w]orkers will be motivated by setting goals and objectives for both the individual and the organization." Other theories similarly explore the influences of money on workplace performance (Fisher, 2009).

Cherry, K. (n.d.). Differences between extrinsic and intrinsic motivation. Retrieved from http://psychology.about.com/od/motivation/f/difference-between-extrinsic-and-intrinsic-motivation.htm

Cherry, K. (n.d.). Theories of motivation. Retrieved from http://psychology.about.com/od/psychologytopics/tp/theories-of-motivation.htm

Cherry, K. (n.d.). What is reinforcement? Retrieved from http://psychology.about.com/od/operantconditioning/f/reinforcement.htm

Čížek, P. (2012). The application of Maslow's hierarchy of needs to the entrepreneur's motivation—The example from region Pardubice. *Scientific Papers of The University of Pardubice. Series D, Faculty of Economics & Administration, 18*(24), 43–50.

Deci, E., Koestner, R., & Ryan, R. (1999). A meta-analytic review of experiments examining the effects of extrinsic rewards on intrinsic motivation. *Psychological Bulletin, 125*(6), 627–668.

Fisher, E. A. (2009). Motivation and leadership in social work management: A review of theories and related studies. *Administration in Social Work, 33*(4), 347–367. doi:10.1080/03643100902769160.

Gollwitzer, P., & Oettingen, G. (2001). Motivation: History of the concept. *International Encyclopedia of the Social & Behavioral Sciences, 15*, 10,109–10,112.

Huitt, W. (2011). Motivation to learn: An overview. educational psychology interactive. Retrieved from http://www.edpsycinteractive.org/topics/motivation/motivate.html

Leddy, C. (2013, October 29). Do employees work harder for higher pay? Retrieved from http://hbswk.hbs.edu/item/7287.html

Maslow, A. (1943). A theory of human motivation. *Psychological Review, 50*, 370–396. Retrieved = from http://psychclassics.asu.edu/Maslow/motivation.htm

McLeod, S. (2007). Skinner—Operant conditioning. Retrieved from http://www.simplypsychology.org/operant-conditioning.html

McLeod, S. (2009). Attachment theory. Retrieved from http://www.simplypsychology.org/attachment.html

Motivation—Definition. (n.d.). Retrieved from http://www.merriam-webster.com/dictionary/motivation

Rana, H. (1997, May 1). Sigmund Freud. *Muskingum University Press*. Retrieved from http://www.muskingum.edu/~psych/psycweb/history/freud.htm

Rynes, S., Gerhart, B., & Minette, K. (2004). The importance of pay in employee motivation: Discrepancies between what people say and what they do. Human Resource Management.

Scholl, R. (2002). What is motivation? *University of Rhode Island*. Retrieved from http://www.uri.edu/research/lrc/scholl/webnotes/Motivation.htm

Thornton, S. (n.d.). Sigmund Freud (1856–1939). *Internet Encyclopedia of Philosophy*. Retrieved from http://www.iep.utm.edu/freud/

credits

Figure 1.1: ED STEIN © 1996 The Rocky Mountain News. Reprinted by permission of Universal Uclick for UFS. All rights reserved.

Figure 6.3: By permission of Dave Coverly and Creators Syndicate, Inc.

index